The North Channel
and
St. Mary's River

a guide to the history

By
Andrea Gutsche
Barbara Chisholm
&
Russell Floren

Copyright 2002 by Lynx Images Inc.
P.O. Box 5961, Station A
Toronto, Canada M5W 1P4
Web Site: http://www.lynximages.com

Editor: Barbara D. Chisholm
Cover design: Jo-Ey Lee
Typesetting and design: Lynx Images Inc.
1st Edition, July 1997
2nd Printing June 2002

Front cover: painting of CPR steamer *Algoma* on St. Mary's River, Artist unknown.
Back cover: Cockburn Island, Lynx Images

Printed and bound in Canada by Metrolitho Inc.
Canadian Cataloguing in Publication Data

Gutsche, Andrea, 1964-
    The North Channel and St. Mary's River: a guide to
the history

Includes bibliographical references and index.
ISBN 1-894073-00-2

1. North Channel Region (Huron, Lake, Mich. and Ont.) -
History.   2. Saint Marys River Region (Mich. and Ont.) -
History.   I. Chisholm, Barbara, 1962-   .   II. Floren,
Russell,   1965-   .   III. Title.

FC3095.N673G87 1997   971.3'132   C97-931320-1
F1059.N63G87 1997

*This book is dedicated to the people of the
North Channel and St. Mary's River*

Ken McColman with old dive gear, Thessalon

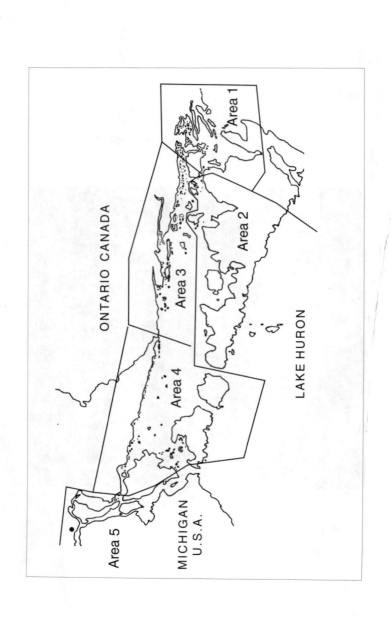

TABLE OF CONTENTS

When trying to locate the sites in this book it is necessary to obtain proper maps and charts for the relevant areas. These will direct you to the sites and away from shoals. The maps in this book are to help the reader gain a sense of the area and are not to be used for navigation.

Every effort has been made to make this book accurate, informative, and useful. While we have scoured the area for stories and interesting information, we do not claim to be doing an exhaustive historical treatment. In condensing complex histories, we are aware of the risk of misrepresenting situations, and hope that our portrayals are found to be fair.

Exploring the North Channel and St. Mary's River is not a simple task, it requires a thorough knowledge of boating, navigation, and, in some cases, diving. Readers should be confident they have the skills with which to safely enjoy their exploration of the area, or they are travelling with someone who does. When going to these sites you do so at your own risk. Lynx Images Inc. takes no responsibility for what might befall you. We have made every effort to note when a site is on or near private property and when permission is required in order to visit a site. Divers must be certified. And we can't stress enough that respect and common sense should always travel with you when on the lakes.

We welcome new stories, updates, information and corrections for subsequent editions. Please write: Lynx Images, P.O. Box 5961, Station A., Toronto, Ontario, M5W 1P4 or visit our web site at

http://www.lynximages.com

Abandoned church on Cockburn Island

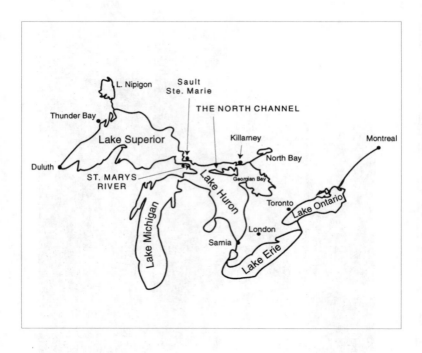

Introduction

The currents that flow through the North Channel and the St. Mary's River are the currents of time. Through the ages these passageways have been an essential artery linking the Upper Great Lakes to Lake Superior, east to west. Perhaps too often they have only been seen as a conduit offering passage from one place to another. Yet it is precisely because these waters were a "highway" that many important themes in Canadian and American history were played out along their shores: westward exploration, the fur trade, French-English tensions, the Iroquois Wars, transportation, boom and bust settlement, the Canada/U. S. border.

It is also a landscape of great beauty. The island-studded ribbon of water stretches from the ancient quartzite hills of

La Cloche, along the North Shore's Precambrian rock. It winds past the limestone wonder of Manitoulin Island (the largest freshwater island in the world), and up the historic St. Mary's River to its source, the magnificent Lake Superior. Great lengths of the route appear pristine, yet as often is the case, appearances are deceiving: this is, in fact, a well-worn passageway. Through the years its waters have been crowded with native and voyageur canoes, cargo-laden schooners, passenger steamers, tugs pulling log booms and freighters loaded with grain and ore.

Many who ventured through here were simply passing through—the crews on ships, immigrants bound for the great Prairie expanse, and single men in search of a living in mining and lumbering. Inevitably, some of the transients stayed. One family who decided to put down roots was the Turners of Little Current, Elizabeth and Isaac. When their steamer made a stop at Little Current, Elizabeth turned to her husband and said, "You can keep heading west but I'm staying right here."

From its earliest years, the region was also a meeting place. Indian bands from Georgian Bay, Michigan and Superior converged at the St. Mary's Rapids for the annual whitefish run; traders exchanged stories and furs; settlers shared food, supplies and gossip while British soldiers from the Drummond Island garrison snowshoed in the dead of winter to visit their counterparts at Fort Brady. From small communities all along the North Shore came baseball teams to play at isolated John Island. For much of the time, the British or Canadian/American border existed in name only as the isolation dictated co-operation and accommodation rather than opposition and confrontation.

This book is an invitation to explore this "water highway," to revisit colourful moments in history, and to revel in the adventures, follies and aspirations of the cast of characters who peopled it.

GEOLOGICALLY SPEAKING . . .

From Oozing Magma to Tropical Seas

More than 3.8 billion years ago, the earth was in ferment, shaken by earthquakes and bathed in poisonous gasses. There was no atmosphere and no life. From deep within its core, hot magma gushed to the surface and crystallised to form the Precambrian Province that includes the regions of Lake Superior, the St. Mary's River and the North Shore. This rock, though often hidden far beneath the soil, forms the foundation of North America.

A billion years passed. Slowly the rock wore down and La Cloche became a vast region of sand. In another billion years this sand turned into stone. Even though none of the earth's continents had yet formed, the plates of the earth were in constant motion, shifting and colliding. One of these collisions generated such intense heat that the sandstone of La Cloche was transformed into quartzite, and under monumental pressure, it folded and buckled until its craggy peaks towered like the Alps.

Around 450 million years ago North America was part of one giant continent called Pangaea with the equator running right though Manitoulin Island! At this time, the North Shore was dramatically altered by two shallow tropical seas, the Ordovician and the Silurian. The Ordovician Sea covered much of southern Ontario with its northern boundary at Birch Island. Limestone deposits that built up over millions of years on her muddy floor, are evident on Goat Island, Great La Cloche, Birch Island and the Manitowaning area of Manitoulin Island.

Some of the tiny tropical creatures of the second sea, the Silurian, were reef builders and have left evidence of their work in the form of peculiar knolls of limestone protruding from farmers' fields near Manitowaning. The most impressive reef, however, is the monolithic arc of limestone known as the Bruce Peninsula that divides Georgian Bay from Lake Huron. Geologists believe that this peninsula once extended all the way to Manitoulin Island.

Between the North Shore and Manitoulin Island, two great geological and geophysical provinces meet: the Precambrian Shield plate rock and the great limestone Palaeozoic Plain. It is possible to see the line where the two butt up against each other on Heywood and Great La Cloche Islands, as well as at Sheguiandah on Manitoulin Island, where the limestone was ground away during the Ice Age, leaving an outcropping of quartzite.

The Ice Age

The Ice Age began 18,000 years ago. Advancing and retreating glaciers slowly ground their way across the Great Lakes. The last to exert its tremendous force over the region was the Wisconsin. Then, 13,000 year ago, the earth started to warm up and the ice began its slow retreat from the Great Lakes. At times the water levels were so high, only the tops of Manitoulin and La Cloche could be seen above the surface. When the seas subsided, the first humans came into the area.

The First Peoples

At Sheguiandah on Manitoulin Island, there is an ancient quartzite quarry used 9,000 years ago by humans we call the Plano. It is possible to build a profile of these people based on the tools, weapons, utensils and fire pits they left behind. For instance we know that the Plano survived by hunting mastodon and caribou with quartzite spears.

The next period of human habitation extends from 5,000-500 B.C. These Archaic people were nomads who used dugout canoes, fish traps, bait fishing and harpoons. They are thought to be the first to have fashioned axes, pendants and spears out of copper. The next evidence of habitation, decorated pottery and net fishing, point to the Middle Woodland period extending from A.D. 500-800. We know even more about the more recent Late Woodland period between A.D. 800-1600. Water transportation improved and fishing moved offshore into areas of deep water; at the semi-permanent summering villages along shorelines and river mouths, evidence of stone-lined trenches used for drying fish has been discovered.

The First Nations People

The First Nations people most commonly associated with the North Channel and St. Mary's are the Ojibwe, the Odawa (Ottawa) and the Potawatomi. They are all part of the same Algonquin linguistic family and call themselves *Anishnaabe* meaning "original men." Oral history suggests that the Ojibwe, Odawa and Potawatomi (who together form the Confederation of Three Fires) began as one people living beside the Atlantic Ocean, the "Great Salt Sea." Acting on instructions delivered in a vision, they moved to the Great Lakes where they split up geographically: the Potawatomi went to Lake Michigan, the Ojibwe to Bawating at Sault Ste. Marie, and the Odawa settled at Michilimackinac and Manitoulin Island.

The Odawa practised the same hunting, fishing and trading economy of other Great Lakes people but were the first of the group to enter the fur trade working for the French alongside the Huron. They fled west after Huronia was destroyed by the Iroquois.

The Ojibwe was the largest and most powerful of the Great Lakes nations and was arguably one of the most powerful in North America. Outstanding hunters and trappers, they ranged from the Great Lakes to the edge of the Prairies. They were a generally peaceful people but could turn into fierce warriors if put to the test.

One of the seasonal foods relied upon was maple syrup.

In the United States, the Ojibwe are called Chippewa. The two words "Ojibwe" and "Chippewa" may have been derived from the Algonquin word *otchipwa* "to pucker" referring to the gathered seams of their moccasins. Ojibwe writer Basil Johnson believes the name Chippewa was given to the people by the Cree who thought their manner of speech was *Chippewae* meaning "he who stammers, slurs and mumbles." The name Ojibwe may have evolved from the mispronunciation of *O-jib-i-weg*, a term that means "those who make pictographs." The Ojibwe's painted pictographs on rock and birchbark scrolls show them to be among the few early North American Indian groups to employ a form of writing.

The large Ojibwe family included the 1,300-strong Mississauga, who in this region lived at the mouth of the Mississagi River and on Manitoulin Island; and the Saulteur, who were traditionally associated with the St. Mary's Rapids at Sault Ste. Marie. After European contact, the Ojibwe became so important to the French fur trade that their language was the unofficial trade language of the northern Great Lakes.

The Coming of Europeans: The Iroquois Wars

Europe cast its eye upon North America and saw there a wealth of natural resources, ripe for exploitation. Most specifically it saw furs. In the early 1600s, fur traders from New France began flooding into the St. Lawrence region, bringing cut-throat competition. To impose order, the French Crown granted trading monopolies to certain individuals who promised to lay claim to any new lands in the name of France.

In July 1615, Samuel de Champlain, cartographer, explorer and later governor of New France, arrived at Georgian Bay and established a trading alliance with the Huron and Odawa. They became the middlemen between the French and the Indian nations on the North Shore and St. Mary's River. As trade and contact increased, the Indians became more and more dependent on European goods and entwined in a changing balance of economic and political power. The French-allied Huron and British-allied Iroquois were already fierce competitors when, in 1640, things came to a head. Because the fur-bearing regions of the St. Lawrence and Lower Lakes were slowly being depleted, the Iroquois initiated a fierce campaign to take over the beaver-rich Upper Great Lakes.

The Iroquois Wars were a series of conflicts ranging from small skirmishes to bloody battles involving thousands of warriors. Fear swept over the region as Indians were ambushed, their villages attacked. This reign of terror affected even the French settlements, as shown in this 1644 letter, " . . . one can travel in the settlement only in armed bands or in barques armed with cannon and soldiers . . . The beauty of the country is now only to be looked at from afar. One can hardly gather greens in a garden for a salad in safety, and in order to get any supplies of wood everyone has to go in battle order or stand guard."

Despite the turmoil, France was determined to extend its control and to make new converts to the Catholic faith. In 1638, Jean Nicolet, an agent for the Company of New France, journeyed to Lake Superior and Michigan to establish trade relations. Meanwhile Recollect and later Jesuit missionaries set out to explore the hinterland and to save

Ojibwe Pipe and Tomahawk dance

souls. The experiences of the "Black Robes" have been documented in a series of volumes called the *Jesuit Relations*. Their purpose, as compiled from letters and diaries, was to further immigration to the New World. But some of these accounts were hardly a glowing endorsement. The priests were ill prepared for the harsh, foreign environment. Among their privations and desperate survival measures were eating boiled lichen or moccasins. In one of the most extreme cases, Father Louys André, who operated a mission on the Mississagi River between 1670-71, was reduced to eating the glue from book bindings.

The year 1649 was a turning point both for the missionaries and the region as a whole. The once-proud Huron nation which before 1600 had numbered around 23,000 had been decimated by disease and by Iroquois attacks. The three hundred Huron remaining in 1649 dispersed. Some joined the Odawa on Manitoulin Island, some spread into Petun country on Georgian Bay, and the rest abandoned their homeland for Quebec. The Iroquois shifted their attention to the Ojibwe and Odawa.

To the Iroquois' surprise, the Ojibwe were not the same easy targets as the Huron who had settled in large villages. Armed only with stone tomahawks, bow and arrow, clubs, and their expertise in guerrilla warfare, the Ojibwe defeated the mighty Iroquois.

The constant warring, exacerbated by devastating epidemics, took a toll on many of the nations. The Odawa and the Ojibwe both left Manitoulin and, in the latter part of the war, the Ojibwe abandoned both the North Channel and St. Mary's. This area became a no man's land. Oral tradition tells that before the Indians departed, they set Manitoulin on fire to rid it of the smallpox brought by the Iroquois.

Throughout the war there were several failed treaty attempts between the French and Iroquois. Finally, in 1701, after a special council in Montreal attended by fifteen Nations, the debilitated Iroquois finally agreed to a truce.

The Fur Trade: The Hudson's Bay Company

In 1656, with the Huron middlemen eradicated, unlicenced French fur traders pushed west along the North Channel and into Lake Superior. Among the first to arrive were Pierre-Esprit Radisson and Médard Chouart des Groseilliers. After amassing a huge stash of furs they returned to Quebec where the pelts were promptly confiscated by the governor as punishment for operating without a licence. They were thrown in jail and forbidden to return to the Lake Superior region. This was not just a matter of a licencing issue. The governor, Pierre de Voyer d'Argenson, feared that further western exploration might shift the focus away from the St. Lawrence and Quebec. Ironically, his actions actually hastened the very situation he had hoped to avoid. In 1665, Radisson and Groseilliers went to Britain to meet with Prince Rupert, a cousin of King Charles II. They offered to explore the fur-rich region beyond Lake Superior with the intention of discovering an entirely new trading route. This meeting laid the groundwork for the establishment of the Hudson's Bay Company.

In 1670, the new Company built several forts along major rivers leading into James Bay and Hudson Bay and encouraged the Indians to come to them to trade. To offset Britain's creeping influence in the region, in 1671, the French moved to take formal possession of the continent's interior by staging an elaborate pageant at the mission on the St. Mary's Rapids. The man sent to represent the king was the son of a Parisian courtier, Simon-François Daumont, Sieur de Saint Lusson. The fourteen nations attending the elaborate ceremony were informed that they were now under the protection of Louis XIV—a significant statement in light of the continued warring of the British-allied Iroquois. To reinforce their position, the French proceeded to build a series of fur trading forts in the region.

The British Unwelcome

The outcome of the 1759 Battle of Quebec dramatically changed the political landscape of the region. Fort Michilimackinac, built by the French on the shores of

Lake Michigan in 1715, became a British possession. The Ojibwe, who had supported the French in this crucial war were loath to see the enemy move into their lands. British fur traders were often attacked by angry natives demonstrating their continued allegiance to France. The first recorded British trader in the Upper Lakes, Alexander Henry, managed to pass through the region unmolested only by dressing as a French voyageur. British condescension and arrogance were part of the problem. Their approach was in sharp contrast to French traders many of whom had married Indian women and assimilated in other ways. However, the strongest factor against the British was a deep-rooted fear that the establishment of British military forts was a first step toward confiscation of Indian lands.

The resentment culminated in Pontiac's Rebellion of 1763-4. Ojibwe, Odawa, and Mississauga were among those who joined in a plot to capture eleven British forts between Pittsburgh and Green Bay. They succeeded in taking nine. Their most famous attack was at Fort Michilimackinac. While playing a game of lacrosse outside the palisade walls, Ojibwe warriors deliberately tossed the ball into the fort. When the gates were opened to return the ball, the Ojibwe flooded in. The garrison was taken off guard; seventy of the ninety soldiers were killed and the rest captured. In 1780, the fort was moved to cliff-lined Mackinac Island, strategically located in the narrows between Lakes Huron and Michigan. Eventually the Ojibwe accepted the British presence, and traded freely with British traders.

Rival Fur Companies
The North West Company is born

In 1783, a group of Montreal-based French and Scottish entrepreneurs banded together to create the North West Company. Their goal, to halt the flow of furs to Hudson Bay. In contrast to the passive approach of the Hudson's Bay Company, waiting for the Indians to come to them with pelts, the aggressive North West Company dispatched traders into the interior to deal directly with the Indians. Their route took them from Montreal, via the French River to Georgian Bay, through the North Channel and on to the far end of Superior and beyond. To provide support for the brigades of voyageurs and passengers, the company set up a series of trading and supply posts on the Great Lakes including Sault Ste. Marie, St. Joseph Island, Drummond Island, Mississagi River and Great La Cloche Island. Eventually, moving westward, the NWC created the first transcontinental trading system in Canada.

Along with the HBC and the NWC, there was also the South West Company, based out of Mackinac Island, as well as a number of smaller trading groups. Rival companies entered into a "no holds barred" competition. In *Caesars of the Wilderness*, Peter C. Newman describes the competition for beaver pelts growing so intense that

> the northern reaches of America's forests became a
> battleground. Both sides settled their accounts in
> blood. Snipers rode the riverbanks. Loaded cannon

were used to reclaim stolen cargoes. Murder and ambush, arson and theft, kidnapping and destruction of property became so common that the act of maiming a competitor was regarded as a condition of doing business.

More devastating than their effects on each other were the effects of the fur trade on Indian society. Many in the Indian population lost their traditional skills and were forced to depend on traders and their goods. Liquor became the currency of choice. Although the HBC was initially against the whiskey trade, they changed their policy in order to remain competitive. The NWC, on the other hand, had no qualms about promoting alcohol as illustrated by the following NWC official's journal excerpt in *Caesars of the Wilderness*, "The love of rum is their first inducement to industry, they undergo every hardship and fatigue to procure a Skinfull of this delicious beverage, and when a Nation becomes addicted to drinking, it affords a strong presumption that they will soon become excellent hunters."

One travelling priest left a chilling account of the effects of alcohol on a couple living along the North Channel. On his first visit, the priest found their wigwam to be clean and carefully tended. Eighteen months later the couple was destitute, "Every part of the wigwam was ruinous and dirty, all the useful and ornamental furniture which eighteen months fore had seemed a source of pride and pleasure was gone and, with the solitary exception of a single kettle, all was dreary desolate and empty." A trader had tricked the Indian trapper into taking a first drink, then continued to ply him with alcohol for three weeks until his entire winter supply of furs was gone. The couple sold everything they owned including the guns and traps on which their livelihood depended. Motivated by compassion, the priest gave them money for food. Soon after he found the man dead in the grass, having drunk himself to death.

Forts—Pawns in a Chess Game

At the conclusion of the American War of Independence (1776-83), diplomats met in Paris to draw up the Treaty of Paris which addressed the division of Indian lands despite the fact that no native peoples were represented at the proceedings. The British argued for an Indian buffer state between the British and Americans in order for the fur trade to continue unimpeded. Known for its strategic significance in control of the fur trade, the British garrison stayed on at Mackinac Island until 1794 when Jay's Treaty enforced the new American border. Reluctantly, the soldiers moved to St. Joseph Island in British territory (see map p.221).

The British soldiers were not the only ones affected. The North West Company trading post located at the Michigan Sault grudgingly moved across the St. Mary's to the Canadian shore, virtually uninhabited swampland. Life in the Canadian Sault was decidedly bleak and for years its residents had to depend on the Americans for provisions and mail.

Far away in Europe, the Napoleonic Wars were about to draw the region into another conflict, the War of 1812. A war virtually nobody wanted. Britain was accused of violating the maritime rights of the neutral United States by boarding ships and harassing American sailors, and by

Indians at the annual present-giving ceremony, Drummond Island Fort in distance

seizing vessels for trading with the enemy. Finding the situation intolerable, on June 18, 1812, the United States Congress declared war on Great Britain. The pivotal role of the Upper Great Lakes in this contest was quickly realized and sleepy Fort St. Joseph, the garrison at the end of the line, sprang into action.

Along with Indian warriors and voyageurs, in July 1812 the garrison launched a pre-emptive attack on Fort Michilimackinac. The Americans were literally caught sleeping, having received no word of the onset of war. (Ironically, it was through American John Jacob Astor that Britain's Fort St. Joseph had been informed. A large quantity of Astor's furs was stashed there and he wanted to protect them!) The Indian nations actively supported the British effort, and their powerful forces no doubt affected the course of history. As pointed out by John Askin Jr., Interpreter-Clerk for the British, "without the Indians we never could keep this country, and with them the Americans will never take the upper posts . . . for in the woods, one Indian is equal to three white men." This indeed proved true during the Americans' unsuccessful attempt to retake Fort Michilimackinac in 1814. A small group of Indian snipers hidden in the forest repelled the attack, killing fourteen and wounding fifty.

Although the War of 1812 ended inconclusively for Britain and the United States, it left the Ojibwe vulnerable to American resentment and retaliation. Chief Ocaita on Drummond Island lamented,

> My heart now fails me. I can hardly speak. We are now slaves and treated worse than dogs. Those bad spirits [the Americans] take possession of our lands without consulting us . . . they even tie us up and torture us almost to death. Our Chiefs did not consent to have our lands given to the Americans [in the Treaty of Ghent], but you did it without consulting us; and in doing that you delivered us to their mercy. They are enraged at us for having joined you in the play.

After the war, the British garrison was once again pushed out of Michilimackinac, and for a second time, the American flag was hoisted above her palisades. Unable to return to the razed Fort St. Joseph, the dispossessed British relocated instead to Drummond Island. Financially strained and weary after years of war with France and America, Britain began to lose interest in her Great Lakes garrisons. Fort Drummond suffered from neglect and from desertion as frustrated soldiers tried to escape to a better life. The high cost of the gift-giving ceremonies with the Indians on Drummond Island came under fire, but the fort Commandant knew the essential strategic value of keeping the Indians as active allies on the western flank of British North America.

After an 1816 law prevented British merchants from trading on American territory, those Ojibwe and Odawa determined to remain trading partners with Britain were forced to move to Canadian soil. The Americanization of the Upper Great Lakes had begun. One of the first to take advantage of this trading opportunity was John Jacob Astor and his renamed American Fur Company. So successful was he that upon his death in the early 1830s, Astor was one of the richest men in America (if not particularly couth: one unimpressed host complained, "He dined here last night and ate his ice cream and peas with a knife").

Determined to break the British stronghold on the fur trade, in 1820 Michigan Governor Lewis Cass travelled by canoe from the Mississippi to Lake Superior to negotiate with the Indians for land to build Fort Brady on the St. Mary's River. His journey, however, gave support to more than the fur trading interests. His imagination was caught by a 3,708 lb. copper boulder at Ontonagon, Lake Superior. No longer would this region be renowned only for its furs. As other mineral resources would be discovered, it became increasingly clear that traders and Indians did not fit into the new picture.

The Treaties

In the 1830s, both Canada and the United States pursued campaigns to remove Indians from their traditional lands and settle them on reservations. In 1836 the British government convinced Manitoulin Indians to sign a treaty that would open the island to Indians from other settled parts of Upper Canada (Ontario). The idea was to turn the island into a giant reserve, thus isolating the natives from growing white settlements. Indian Agent Thomas G. Anderson chose Manitowaning on Manitoulin Island for the site of an educational centre where Indians could be taught trades and farming, to wean them off their traditional lifestyle. Ironically, when Anderson and a group of white settlers and teachers arrived at Manitoulin in the autumn of 1838, they would not have survived the winter were it not for the Indians who taught them the very skills the government hoped them to abandon.

These schemes failed because many Indians refused to relocate to Manitoulin. Of those that made the move, the majority were from the U. S. and had supported the British in the War of 1812. They moved expressly to preserve their traditions, not to replace them.

Efforts to convert the natives to Christianity had continued since the Jesuits arrived in the 1600s. Rivalries among the different faiths developed, which confused rather than attracted the natives. In one instance, the Anglican Reverend Charles Brough of Manitowaning who spoke no Ojibwe, removed his Indian interpreter, Assiginack, because he was on friendly terms with the Catholic priest Father Proulx from Wikwemikong. Troubled by the conflicting messages the churches were sending his people, Hereditary Chief Shingwauk canoed all the way to Toronto seeking government assistance.

> We had been visited by several different Black-coats, and their talking seemed to be different one from another. The French Black-coat [Roman Catholic]

> wanted us to worship God his way; the English
> Black-coat wanted us to follow his religion; and
> there was another Black-coat who took the people,
> dipped them right into the water, and he wanted us
> all to join him.

Lieutenant Governor Colborne resolved the situation by sending a young missionary from the Church of England to reside among Shingwauk's people.

In the early 1830s, the North Channel and St. Mary's regions were still Indian territory, plied mainly by native and voyageur canoes. This was about to change. The fur trade was on the wane and was being replaced by industries for which the Indians were no longer necessary. More and more schooners appeared, followed in the late 1830s by the first steamships.

As industrialization took hold, North America developed an insatiable hunger for minerals. That 3,708-pound Ontonogan copper boulder had sparked a staking rush. At Bruce Mines, the bonanza discovery of a copper vein in 1846 created the first mining town in Ontario. Even though native lands were officially protected by the Royal Proclamation of 1763, overzealous prospectors and mining companies ignored their boundaries and set up mines. Such behaviour sent Chief Shingwauk from Garden River to assert his rights and chase miners off Indian land on Lake Superior in 1849. He and the Chief from Batchawana were arrested and detained in a Toronto prison. They were safe from prosecution however, as it was obvious the miners had been trespassing. A year later, two treaties were signed, the Robinson-Huron Treaty, covering the north shore of Lake Huron including the North Channel and St. Mary's, and the Robinson-Superior Treaty covering Lake

Superior. The treaties set up small reserves; secured Indian hunting and fishing rights (except where the government had already given those rights to others); and set out an annuity of one pound per person which would increase if the province of Ontario ever made a profit from the surrendered lands. A Lake Superior Chief complained in 1852,

> Father, you said to the Indians: My Children, you have no need of strangers to manage your business. I am your father, you are my children: you should have confidence in me . . . And we believed you; we placed our name on your paper without knowing what it contained. We thought that what was written on your paper was the same as your heart.

It was too late. The face of the region was dramatically altered.

The New Era: Settlement

The 1850s and 1860s accelerated activity in the region. The U.S. State Lock opened formally linking Lake Superior to the Great Lakes network; railways from the south-east reached several Great Lakes ports; and settlers arrived. Once again, the government turned its eyes toward Manitoulin Island.

In 1862, the Indians were induced to sign yet another treaty, this time opening Manitoulin to general settlement. They were placed on reserves based on religious and community ties. Wikwemikong, West Bay, and Shesheguaning were Roman Catholic. Sucker Creek and Sheguiandah were Anglican. A traditional Ojibwe and Odawa community was established at Obidgewong. There was one hold-out: the Wikwemikong Chiefs refused to sign. To this day, Wikwemikong is Canada's only unceded reserve. Several confrontations ensued between the settlers and people from Wikwemikong. In 1863, fearing a Wikwemikong uprising, the government sent in twenty-two armed regulars. Father Kohler, who had urged the Wikwemikong Chiefs to assert themselves, was arrested and a government agent murdered.

On the American shores, proceedings were no better. At an 1855 final treaty conference in Detroit, Chippewa from the Sault strongly protested that the locks had destroyed their village and an historical fishing site that had been promised to them in perpetuity in earlier treaties.

All over the region, the floodgates had lifted and the settlers poured in. The 1868 Free Grants and Homestead Act encouraged Canadian settlement by offering each family 200 acres, with an extra 100 acres for each child over eighteen. The quality of the land varied widely. Settlers

Ojibwe houses alongside the lock. Not only did lock construction destroy their original homes but also much of their fishery.

Lumbering was serious business. When a saw-filer was seen charging out of a Mississagi River lumber camp, a French-Canadian logger explained to his boss, "He do no good job. I chase him. I don't kill him. I should 'ave."

attracted to Cockburn Island for the cheap land found the soil incapable of sustaining long-term farming. In contrast, St. Joseph Island, with its rich soil and moderate climate was crowned the "Garden of Algoma." According to *Trade History of the North Shore*, by 1901 there were 4,673 farms in Algoma producing thousands of tons of livestock, vegetables, eggs, jam, dried fruit and feed.

The Industries: Logging

As Lake Michigan's lumber resources were depleted, American sawmill firms turned to the bounty of the North Channel's North Shore and purchased Crown timber limits in yearly auctions. While most of the logs were towed to the U.S. to be milled, mills of varying sizes sprang up all along the North Shore and the St. Mary's. Lumbering was an important local industry which kept farmers, fishermen and even sailors employed during the long winter.

In 1878, Canadian companies were hit by an increased import tax on sawmill machinery purchased in the U.S. In retaliation, Canada placed an export tax on Canadian logs towed across the border. The United States responded with the Dingley Tariff Act placing a tax on milled lumber from Canada. This caused a number of North Shore mills to close. Two years later, Canada raised the stakes by banning the export of any logs cut on Crown land. The Americans acknowledged defeat. Michigan companies had no choice but to unscrew the bolts on their mills and tow them to Canada. The golden age of logging on the North Shore had begun.

Each spring, the North Shore's river systems were clogged with timber. The river drive was particularly dangerous and workers were at the mercy of uncaring owners. Former logger Charlie Quinn:

> There was no such thing as unions. No such thing as an eight hour day . . . . Men were paid by the month. When they upped the hours (during the river drive) you didn't get more money. Sometimes the company would pay towards looking after you if you got hurt but sometimes you were on your own. A lot of people got broken legs and killed . . .

In *In Days of Old: Experiences of an Early Algoma Settler*, S. C. Gardiner wrote of his experiences working a small mill on the Serpent River in 1873. One year he went for five months without pay despite the many promises made by the owner. Gardiner remembers another occupational hazard: the bugs. "I believe the Serpent River could and did produce more black flies and mosquitoes to the square inch than any other place I have been in." He describes one man who was so badly bitten that he laid down on a path and might have died if another man had not come along. "He was a terrible looking object when he got back. His neck, face and chest were all covered with blood."

Fishing

With local waters filled with whitefish, herring and pickerel, fishing had always been a major industry. Two remarkable fisheries "bookended" the region, both chronologically and physically: the old St. Mary's Rapids fishery where, hundreds of years before, native groups had gathered to enjoy the annual whitefish run; and Killarney, which evolved from a fur-trading post into one of the busiest fishing communities on the North

Early nets were made by unraveling linen cloth, then knitting them by hand.

Shore. In between, the North Channel was dotted with dozens of fishing communities such as Meldrum Bay, Thessalon, Cockburn Island, Desbarats and Blind River. This was one industry where a man could be his own boss, and several smaller camps were established on islands like John and Fishery, many of which still bear remnants of dock cribs and pilings.

Fishing hit its peak in the 1890s. Canadian fishermen were forced to align themselves with an American buyer as a result of the 1891 American McKinley Tarrif which placed a tax on Canadian fresh fish brought into the United States. Almost all fishermen on the North Channel sold their fish to either the Detroit Fish Company, the Buffalo Fish Company or the Booth Fish Company of Chicago who could circumvent the tax by claiming their product was American.

Shipping

As roads were poor, logging companies, fishermen, mining companies and farmers all depended on the waterways to connect them to their markets. The 1880s to the turn of the century was the golden age of the steamship. Wood-fuelling then coal-fuelling docks popped up at every bend. It was a lucrative business open to all and for an especially enterprising settler, the captive customers offered almost limitless possibilities for added income. Extra cords of wood added to the lading bill secretly turned up on board as whiskey. By the end of the century the fate of the schooners had long been sealed, first by the sidewheeler, then by propeller-driven ships. Unable to meet the increasing demand for speed and efficiency required for the short

Head-candles not only provided light for miners at Bruce Mines but also the time it took for the candle to burn down marked the length of one shift.

shipping season, the once romantic schooners were relegated to scow status, towed to their destinations by the new lords of the lake.

The North Shore was alive with passenger and provision boats running back and forth to serve the new lumber camps, fishing centres, mining camps, produce and cattle depots and the Canadian Pacific Railway construction sites. Tourism was on the rise with excursions to the Sault from Cleveland and Detroit. Boats such as the *Illinois* and *City of Cleveland* offered brass bands and half rates for children and servants. The Anchor Line's new iron ships, the *India, China* and *Japan* lured passengers with promises of elegant interiors, featuring fine furniture and crystal chandeliers. To share in this burst of tourism, the Canadian Pacific Railway launched its own passenger-freight line in 1884 with the *Alberta, Algoma* and *Athabasca.* For a few years, Algoma Mills on the North Channel was the railhead for freight to be shipped via the steamers to the Lakehead.

During the shipping boom in the 1890s, two new competing companies emerged: the Great Northern Transit Company (remembered for the ill-fated *Asia* and *Manitoulin*) and the North Shore Navigation Company. The two were nicknamed the White Line and the Black Line respectively, for their distinctive colouration. The *Asia's* usual route carried it from Sarnia, along the North Shore past Manitoulin Island, Cockburn Island and Thessalon then on to the Sault.

As competition increased, captains were apt to push operations to the limit. Passengers became increasingly put off by the harried pace and mistreatment. Faced with yet another unscheduled stop at Richards Landing, the captain

The State Lock opened Lake Superior to Great Lakes shipping

of the Great Northern Transit Company's *Pacific* forced two passengers to jump off onto the dock while the ship was still moving. Also on the list of passenger complaints was the poor condition of some vessels.

J. D. Dobie's column in the *Bruce Mines Herald* describes a ride on the steamer *Africa*,

> . . . There were too many people on board to be properly fed and riots occurred . . . To add to the misery and delay, quite a number of the bodies from the wrecked steamer [Asia] were picked up at intervals along the bay, causing much nervousness among the passengers.

The steamer *Asia* had foundered in 1882 resulting in over 120 deaths. With the ship overcrowded with provisions, livestock and passengers, her captain had ignored a barometric warning and set out into what became a hurricane force storm. The loss of the *Asia* was a milestone in Canadian Great Lakes marine history. Out of the subsequent government inquiry came a hydrological survey of the Lakes' rocks and shoals and the construction of a series of lighthouses.

The first lighthouses to be built on the Canadian waters of the North Channel around the time of Canadian Confederation were in key locations like Killarney, Little Current, Spider Island and Clapperton Island. The functional square lighthouses were a great improvement to the makeshift navigational aids previously set up by the locals. One of the more enterprising methods was described by Reverend Kingsley Joblin as he rode in a ship's wheelhouse through the St. Mary's,

> when one buoy had been passed and no others were in sight, it was necessary for the helmsman to turn

his back to the wheel and keep the last two markers
in line until the officer could find the next one ahead.
It gave one a strange feeling to be steaming ahead
inwhile the helmsman was looking out the window
behind!

The combination of the North Channel and the St.
Mary's River was a formidable obstacle for any ship's captain. The North Channel route earned the nickname "the
Turkey Trail" because of the sight of ships ducking in and
around islands and shoals. The St. Mary's was so fraught
with currents, shoals and rapids that it was considered
more of an obstacle course than a river. Furthermore, the
waters were crowded with huge booms of logs being
towed to mills along the shores. Many ships would wait at
Sailors Encampment for morning or fair weather before
attempting the run. But a few Captains with strong nerves
(and deadlines on which their careers depended) would
tempt the fates at night if they had the services of a local
pilot such as "Nighthawk" William Greenough whose
uncanny ability to avoid treacherous shoals was legendary.

It took until 1892 to erect fifteen lighthouses on Lake
George to guide ships through the channel. At that point,
plans were already underway to dredge the passageway. At
the turn of the century when dredging work was completed, the lighthouses were discarded.

Today, the St. Mary's River continues to be a traffic
thoroughfare for freighters hauling cargo to and from
Thunder Bay, Duluth and other Superior ports. But the
North Channel shipping route has been passed over. First
came the railway, then improved roads and a car bridge to
Manitoulin. The final blow came with the growth of the
trucking industry which eroded and eventually destroyed

Collisions were cause for concern before ships were separated in up and down bound channels on the St. Mary's River. Here the steel CPR passenger steamer Athabasca *has part of the wooden steamer* Pontiac *on her bow after a collision in the St. Mary's River.*

the need for steamer service. In the 1960s, the *Normac* retired when her wooden cabins failed to meet inspection standards. With it, passenger service ended on the North Channel.

The St. Mary's River and the North Channel have been both participant in and witness to the flow of history. If their waters could speak, many would be the stories they could tell. In the chapters that follow, some of those secrets will be revealed through human memories and human voices.

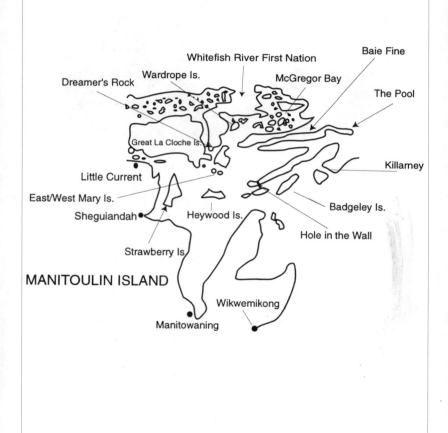

1

KILLARNEY TO STRAWBERRY ISLAND

Early Killarney

Because of the long, protected channel created by George Island, Killarney was known originally as Shebahonaning or "Straight and Narrow Passage." In the 1820s, it was the site of a small independent fur-trading post built by Stephen (Etienne) Augustin Rochbert de la Morandiere and his Indian wife, Josephte Sai-sai-go-no-kwe, "Woman of Falling Snow." Shebahonaning must have been a welcome sight to the many voyageurs, fur traders, missionaries and Indians who arrived. After months of travelling, it may have reminded them of home as they watched the fur trader's ten children playing by the water, laundry flapping in the breeze and cows grazing near a garden of corn, wheat and potatoes.

Morandiere had chosen the location well, for Shebahonaning was the halfway point on the well-travelled trade route between Montreal and Fort William on Lake Superior.

Today Killarney is the oldest permanently-settled community on the North Channel. Many residents are related to the French and Ojibwe inhabitants of that early trading post. Writer Bruce Pitfield has chronicled Killarney's founding families, some of whom were voyageurs, interpreters and strong British allies. The Solomons can trace their roots back to Ezekiel Solomon, the man believed to be Michigan's first Jew. Born in Germany, Ezekiel arrived at Fort Michilimackinac in 1761 as a fur trader. He survived the bloody massacre of 1763 when Pontiac's warriors attacked the British fort, was taken prisoner by the Odawa and ransomed by his captors in Montreal (see p.221 for a map showing Fort Michilimackinac location). In 1841, Honoré (Henry), a relative, arrived at Killarney, still a small settlement of fewer than ten families.

From Furs to Fish

One of the first outside accounts of Killarney comes from the infamous settler (and polygamist), William Kingdom Rains, who passed through on his way to start a colony on St. Joseph Island. On May 13, 1836, he wrote:

> A large assembly of Indians and well dressed Canadians were drawn out to receive us. Two or three volleys were fired. This was a trading post, the first we had seen, and a few drams amply repaid the Indians for the expenditure of their ammunition. In the first evening we were invited to the house of the trader, Mr. Lamarandunt [de la Morandiere], and we danced away to the merry sound of the fiddle with the gay and lively half-breeds.

By the 1890s, Killarney had evolved from trading post to respected fishing station where fishermen worked out of Mackinaw sailing boats and salt-preserved their catches in barrels. A 1979 interview with Jim Lowe mentions his father, who had become a fisherman at the age of twelve.

In the 1830s, steamers like the Gore *brought the outside world to Killarney.*

> He first got his licence from the Dominion of Canada. It was a $10 licence for 60,000 yards [of net]. He could fish anywhere on the Great Lakes . . . When my Dad first started to fish they had to knit their own nets. They didn't have leads for weights; they used stones. And they made their own floats out of cedar.

It was a humble beginning for a settlement that would become renowned for fishing.

Prodigious catches enabled fishermen to own their own tugboats and deliver their bounty directly to the railhead at Collingwood. At its peak at the turn of the century, Killarney was regularly visited by the packet steamers *Manitou* and *Caribou* which hauled five hundred tons of Killarney's fish per season. Jim Lowe recalled that in the 1920s, he would see the *Manitou* arrive around 2:00 p.m., load fish at six or seven docks, then head off to Owen Sound at three in the morning.

Some of the town's most hilarious entertainment came from its "first come, first served" policy. Gordon MacCaulay's memoirs, published in a 1964 edition of *Inland Seas*, recall:

> the lead ship would pick up the bulk of the cargo . . . If a two-hour lead could not be opened up [between ships], an intriguing game of leap frog took place along Killarney's waterfront which consisted of seven docks. The rivals [*Caribou* and *Manitou*] would always give way in time but this little sport did become rough on fenders, guard-rails and the docks themselves. The language hurled between the two ships as a result of these near misses vibrated harshly on delicate ears, male or female.

Struggle With Isolation

Although the name Killarney had been known for years to merchants in the big fish markets of Toronto, Chicago and New York City, its fame soon spread to sport fisher-men who came to appreciate the isolation as well as the fishing. One 1925 visitor was intrigued by Killarney's unique character,

> It has no mayor or reeve or councillors, no taxes except those for its fine school . . . Old French customs prevail. When a younger sister marries, her elder unmarried sister must dance in her stocking feet at the wedding . . . Children pay New Year's calls for the parental blessing as in Old France, and there is much formal visiting for six days . . . Killarney has a custom peculiar to itself and born doubtless of its isolation. On January 6, it elects a king and queen, whose duty it is to provide a social gathering.

Tragedy runs deep in Killarney's blue waters. The lack of road access may have contributed to Killarney's charm, but it also made residents more vulnerable. There is hardly a family without a tragic or near-tragic story about battling the elements. One horrifying event took place in 1888. About a half mile from Killarney, a Captain Foote discovered a dead man lashed to the bowsprit of a foundering sailboat. Foote towed the swamped vessel to Killarney where the man was identified as a local fisherman, Ferdinand Roque Jr. As the boat was examined, a second body was found tied to the rigging. It was the town's schoolteacher. According to a story handed down through the Roque family, the previous night, Foote had dreamt of seeing two men clinging to a foundering sailboat.

As Roque had been an experienced sailor, the catastrophe struck at the heart of Killarney. However, many in the community shared a fatalistic belief that all the

Andy Tyson swims to a drifting boat with an inflated moose stomach, 1934

expertise in the world could not save a person from destiny's grip. Nevertheless, no one was going to give in without a fight. On a hunting trip in 1934, Ferdinand Solomon and Andy Tyson noticed their boat had drifted from shore and was too far away for either of them to safely swim to it. What on earth were they going to do? After a little thought, Tyson suggested blowing into the stomach of their recently-killed moose with a tube of rolled up cigarette paper, and using these "inflatables" to help them swim to the boat.

The desirability of road access took on new meaning in winter. Naturally, except in those areas where currents produced weak ice, the frozen waterway could be used as a road. However, as eighty-seven-year-old retired fisherman Peter Lowe recalls, the only way to avoid dangerous spring ice was to take an incredibly circuitous route via

Rat Portage, over the Baie Fine mountains, across Split Cove Portage to Birch Island, then on to the mainland or Little Current.

Despite much local grumbling, the issue of road access remained dormant until 1923 when eighty-year-old Pierre Regis de la Morandiere (son of Charles) went to Toronto to petition the government. This was only the beginning of almost forty years of lobbying. It wasn't until 1962 that a road was finally built. Although tourists feared cars would ruin Killarney's unspoiled charm, the community had no intention of changing. In 1995, the community celebrated its 175th anniversary with a party that would have made their ancestors proud—much like their 150th anniversary party, after which one participant quipped, "We got started on a Thursday night and I never got to bed until the following Tuesday. And I never woke up until the following Thursday!"

BADGELEY ISLAND

The Wreck of the Burlington

In the early 1850s, Badgeley Island was one of the eleven sites chosen to host the first limestone lighthouses to be built on the shores of Lake Huron, Georgian Bay and the North Channel. However, the construction costs for the first six were so prohibitive, Badgeley Island never received its Imperial tower. It was more than a half century later before a wooden tower and back range light were constructed for the lumber and fishing traffic from Killarney, Collins Inlet, and Little Current.

The 452-foot Burlington *rammed Badgeley Island at full speed.*

Life at a lighthouse was full of surprises, and keeper Ferdinand Solomon had his share. Enjoying a quiet evening with his wife Merle, Ferdinand felt the house shake as if an earthquake had struck. Looking out the window, he shouted in a stunned voice, "My God Merle! There's a ship on our verandah!" There sat the *Burlington*, ablaze in lights, looming up against the night sky.

The *Burlington*, a 452-foot, 8,500-ton bulk freighter had been heading back to the Lakehead after unloading grain at Midland. It was nearing the end of season, and the rush was on. They had just come down from the Lakehead in a fierce storm, and as they started up Georgian Bay the storm was still blowing across Lake Huron. Rather than cutting across the exposed northern end of the lake, Captain N. J. Gildner decided to take the more protected North Channel route. More protected, but more hazardous.

Merrill Moore, fireman on board that October 26, 1949, recalls that it had been a miserable day of sleet, snow, rain, and wind. It was 10:30 p.m. and there was a palpable tension in the wheelhouse. The plan was to get in behind the islands, drop the hook and wait until daylight. Through the haze they spotted the dim lights of the Badgeley Island range, but were they near or far? Very near as it turned out. With an horrific gnashing sound the huge freighter piled up on a forty-foot rock ledge directly below the Badgeley Island lighthouse. "The wheelsman and watchman who slept forward, they piled out of bed, but in the stern, we didn't even feel it. I was asleep and didn't even know we hit," remembers Moore.

The tug *Favorite* sent from Sault Ste. Marie to refloat the ship, ran aground near Little Current! When it finally arrived, the tug found the ship's hull badly ripped by the rocks. However, with the aid of ballast pumps, the listing *Burlington* was able to ride under her own power to Collingwood. After thirty-five plates were replaced she was ready for the ensuing season.

In 1981, after the automated tower was put in place, Badgeley Island lighthouse was dynamited. Only a rubble-filled foundation remains.

HOLE IN THE WALL

Home to a small fishing station, Hole In The Wall was owned by the Roszel family until they sold their fishing licence around 1944 to Charlie Green from Little Current. It was notorious for its mosquito population. Charlie's son, Gary recalls one unpleasant night when they were so plagued by the pesky hordes that they retreated to their boat and slept amongst the fish. The smell of the fish seemed to work and so they decided to sleep permanently in the old fishing shack. However, it had a leaky roof. The solution? Pitch a tent inside. By 1960 Kenneth Wells' *Cruising the North Channel* referred to the forgotten station as "tumbling twine sheds and ice houses, collapsed and rotten wharves, not safe to walk on." Now there is little evidence that a camp was ever here. *Look for the cribs in the water in the tiny bay on Creak Island. Watch out for poison ivy.*

BAIE FINE

Earth's Incredible Story

Baie Fine is a majestic fjord cutting through ancient white quartzite hills. Clinging to its sheer rock cliffs are determined, gnarled pine with thick, snaking roots, their green spires stark against the bent backs of the tired, bald mountains. The La Cloche mountains, created by tremendous forces unleashed deep in the earth and worn down by time, are among the oldest mountain ranges on earth.

In the beginning, billions of years ago, La Cloche was a region of sand dunes miles thick, washed white as snow. Over millions of years, the sand turned to stone. Here it waited until jolted by the explosive collision of shifting plates along the earth's mantel. Bombarded by heat and pressure, the sandstone was transformed into a 6,000-

foot-thick band of quartzite that folded and buckled and thrust upwards to the surface. La Cloche was born, her towering range as high as the Rocky Mountains. Over the millennia, this once formidable landscape was slowly worn down. Today, the summits of these mountains, only 300 to 1,180 feet above Lake Huron, extend from Killarney west to the mouth of the North Shore's Spanish River.

Into this region, about 10,000 years ago, came groups of early semi-nomadic people—the Plano, as they were subsequently named. They used the local quartzite to carve crude tools and projectiles to hunt the mastodon and giant caribou that roamed freely over the La Cloche hills. Telltale traces of their existence remain along the shores behind Baie Fine. (For more about the formation of the region see Geologically Speaking p.XI. For the Plano see Sheguiandah p.44).

NEHAHUPKUNG/FRAZER BAY HILL

The Creator's Message

It was on the peak of *Nehahupkung*, "Where-the-rocks-ask-you-to-return-to-them," that Shawonoswe, the great Ojibwe chief and healer, was given a glimpse into the future. He had been praying and fasting on Dreamer's Rock when a magnificent white Thunderbird swooped down and commanded him to climb on his back. Through the air they soared, until Shawonoswe was deposited on Nehahupkung. It was no accident that the Thunderbird had chosen Nehahupkung for it was at this mountain that countless generations of Ojibwe had received the Creator's highest teachings.

Suddenly the Creator appeared sitting in a cloud holding a bowl of water. He asked Shawonoswe to look inside. Shawonoswe saw men and animals and without being told, understood what they were thinking and feeling. He saw the coming of pale-faced ones and he saw war. Bewildered, the chief asked the Creator why this should be. The Creator told Shawonoswe that he had been brought to Nehahupkung to learn certain precepts of harmony and order, that the visions he had seen would come to pass but to have faith that his people would survive. The Creator then imparted laws by which Shawonoswe was to rule his people. In addition, he was to erect a large pole made from the tallest cedar tree and conduct a ceremony each spring and fall in honour of the Creator.

As quickly as he had appeared, the Creator vanished. Shawonoswe was left to find his way home alone. He was found at the shore by fishermen who were shocked to find a naked man without a canoe, weapons or food. On his return to his village, Shawonoswe erected the pole as instructed and conducted the appropriate ceremonies. But one autumn, his helpers neglected to carry out his promise. A violent thunderstorm arose and a great lightning bolt struck the pole, shattering it in a great explosion. With deep humility, Shawonoswe instructed the people to erect another pole and to never again forget to honour the Creator.

Shawonoswe's experience on Nehahupkung only

increased the Ojibwe's reverence for this site. The accomplishment of reaching its peak to pray and fast remained an integral part of spiritual life. But the mountain (named Frazer Bay Hill on charts) was threatened in the 1980s. Indusmin Ltd., a subsidiary of Falconbridge Ltd., had registered a claim to mine silica. In an effort to protect the site, the Whitefish River First Nation referred to provisions set out in the North Channel and the North Georgian Bay Recreational Reserve Acts. However, a loophole in the Mining Act gave precedence over preservation. Test drilling commenced.

Citing religious, cultural and historical grounds, the band next appealed to the Ministry of the Environment and Natural Resources. They buttressed their argument with a reminder that the $25 million tourism industry would be negatively affected by the presence of a mine. Indusmin argued that mining and tourism could co-exist and that all appropriate steps would be taken to maintain the scenic beauty of the area. In 1986, Falconbridge was granted surface rights.

Unwilling to give up, the Whitefish River First Nation made a personal plea to Falconbridge. The mountain was to them a holy place of worship. It was profoundly sacred, among the few places in recorded history that could attest to the appearance of the Creator to humankind. The company responded that the glass industry brought $5 million annually into the region and would collapse without the pure quartzite found at Frazer Bay Hill. As a compromise, the company promised to mine only the base of the mountain and to leave the top untouched. The band compared this proposal to cutting away the foundation of the most important cathedral, while preserving its steeple. The situation did not change.

The Council then united forces with other First Nations Councils. The Ministry of Environment and Natural Resources was deluged with 90,000 letters and petitions opposing the mining lease. After eight years of public opposition, Falconbridge Ltd. surrendered its interest in mining claims in the Baie Fine area.

Frazer Bay Hill has been officially renamed Casson's Peak after Group of Seven painter A. J. Casson.

From both sides of the peninsula a path leads up to the summit of Nehahupkung. The Baie Fine side is more demanding and has thicker bush. On the south side of Frazer Point, the rocks are smoother and more open, making it an easier climb. If anchoring, look for a calm day.

The Group of Seven made Baie Fine their headquarters. Franklin Carmichael sketches at Grace Lake, 1935.

THE POOL

Playground for the Rich, Famous and Notorious

Baie Fine's long fjord terminates at The Pool, a sheltered, idyllic cup of water cradled by the surrounding La Cloche mountains. The Pool's tranquil beauty and the expanse of lakes sleeping in the chalk white hills behind her, made visitors and residents passionate about the area.

When the Spanish River Lumber Company started logging the area around 1880, their headquarters were in the rustic brown cabin still standing at The Pool. According to Dorothy Spreadborough-Wilkins, whose father, Newland Spreadborough, worked for the company as a scaler in 1904, there was a second building used for eating and sleeping, along with a cluster of smaller structures for storing hay and dry goods. The residence, completed in 1912, was about fifty-six feet long with beautiful hardwood floors and panelling. It included a kitchen, pantry and rooms for the servants. Lumberjacks entered the dining room through the back door (where Dorothy recalls the "no talking rule" was imposed to forestall fighting) while logging bosses used a private entrance at the front which led to a living room and bedrooms.

The company owned thirty-five logging camps which had to be visited regularly by Newland Spreadborough. He possessed all the qualities—mathematical skill and meticulousness—that a good scaler needed to calculate the number of useable board feet in a tree. As the company had the right to cut all wood varieties, Spreadborough was swamped with information that had to be registered in

Front steps of the Spanish River Lumber Co. headquarters, 1920.
The Spreadboroughs l to r: Christina, Dorothy (baby), Margaret,
Ellen and Newland.

triplicate—one record for the government, another for the
company and one for himself.

After a long winter, Spreadborough was happy to be joined
by his family during the summer months. As soon as school
ended, his wife Christina and three daughters, Dorothy,
Margaret and Ellen would begin their somewhat circuitous
journey by train and boat from Bracebridge via North Bay,
Sudbury and Little Current to Baie Fine. Dorothy recalls the
train "daddled along" to Little Current. She remembers a
more "aromatic" train ride at the end of season: the passenger car was at the tail end of a long string of cattle cars!

As his daughters grew older, Spreadborough decided to
construct a family cabin on the island at the mouth of The
Pool. He wrote the Spanish River Lumber Company for
permission to use the lumber from an abandoned scow

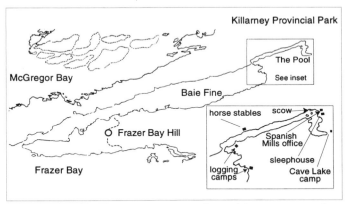

lying near the shore. In 1929, the cabin was completed—all for the price of a two-cent stamp, jokes Dorothy.

The area changed dramatically during Spreadborough's years at The Pool. From a hinterland traversed only by loggers, Indians and trappers, it became a favoured summer playground for the wealthy. The family guest book is scrawled with names such as Count Felix Von Luckner a.k.a. "The Sea Devil," who sent many an Allied vessel to the bottom of the sea in the First World War; American Gutzon Borglum, sculptor of Mount Rushmore; Arctic explorer Donald MacMillan; and the Evinrudes of outboard motor fame. The most notorious was Chicago Mayor William Hale Thompson, remembered for his deeply corrupt administration in the 1920s and his close association with gangster Al Capone.

Big Bill, as everyone called him, glided onto the scene in his palatial yacht, *Doris*. Too large to be brought into Baie Fine, the vessel was anchored in McGregor Bay while Thompson explored the area. He was entranced and later stayed at the company headquarters while purchasing five acres of land at Threenarrows Lake. Dorothy recalls her father's disgust when Big Bill joined the bosses at the breakfast table in nothing but his underwear.

Thompson was a colourful addition to an already eclectic community. His "back to nature" tastes included a giant bedspread made of skunk skins, and a pet bear. Yet he was not one to relish solitude entirely on his own. It was a common sight to see Thompson being trailed by an entourage of goons toting "violin cases," or, in more private moments, enjoying the company of his "personal secretary." "When he died, she sure came out smelling like a rose," Dorothy chuckles. "She got quite a bit of money out of it." At one point, Big Bill decided the size of his property had to match his big passion for La Cloche and so he attempted to buy Baie Fine in its entirety! With the help of their member of Parliament, local residents intervened to block the sale.

The Group of Seven and Killarney Provincial Park

Some of the more welcome guests of the Spreadboroughs were Group of Seven painter Arthur Lismer, his wife Esther and daughter Marjorie. Drawn by Lismer's enthusiasm for the area, his fellow painters, Frank Carmichael, A.Y. Jackson and A. J. Casson quickly fell under the spell of La Cloche and before long, the Group made Baie Fine their headquarters.

A conversation between Newland Spreadborough and A.Y. Jackson in 1931 proved the spark that changed the future of this region. Jackson, his canoe packed with paints and drawing materials, was about to set off on his annual autumn sketching trip when Spreadborough mentioned that the Spanish River Lumber Company planned to log around Jackson's favourite lake. According to Kevin Callan's *Killarney*, Jackson spoke to several people in Toronto about intervening and learned that there was an upcoming naturalists' convention. Shy about public speaking, Jackson wrote an impassioned letter that was read at the conference, and caught the ear of the Minister of Lands and Forests who sprang into action and arranged an exchange of timber rights for the Spanish River Lumber Co.

During the 1950s, the Ontario government woke up to the fact that increasing development was threatening the natural beauty of the Great Lakes region. The province needed to create provincial parks to preserve unique areas and to keep them accessible to the public. After listening to the pleas of a group called Ontario Artists Killarney, the Ministry of Lands and Forests agreed that La Cloche and the North Channel were worthy of   conservation. In 1962, the Killarney Recreational Reserve Act was enacted protecting four thousand square miles of the region's shoreline from development. Amended in 1964, the Act is now the North Georgian Bay Recreational Reserve Act.

Originally, Killarney Provincial Park was to include hiking trails, horseback riding, a golf course and a ski lift at Silver Peaks. Thankfully, this 48,000 hectares of Ontario's finest canoe country has become a wilderness preserve where sensitivity to the environment is the top priority. For more information, write Killarney Provincial Park, Killarney, Ontario, POM 2A0. (705) 287-2368.

MCGREGOR BAY

Captain Alexander McGregor immigrated to Lake Huron from Scotland in the early 1800s and began his Great Lakes career skippering schooners. In 1831 he started his fishing operations out of Main-Station Island in Lake Huron, shipping whitefish and herring to Detroit, Toledo and other Great Lakes ports. The Detroit contract alone called annually for 3,000 barrels of salted fish for which McGregor was paid a dollar a barrel. Unfortunately for him, his success was short-lived.

He had begun fishing in the early years when no fishing licences were needed. This situation changed in the 1840s. Hearing that licences were pending, a few envious locals managed to finangle a licence which gave them a monopoly over McGregor's waters. Their Niagara Fishing Company soon forced him off Main-Station Island. He was pushed out of Lake Huron, and after failing at Tobermory, McGregor moved to Cape Croker.

Far from being a saint himself, McGregor was a trader of questionable ethics who traded liquor for treaty payments. He was also something of a rogue. He abandoned his Caucasian wife and children in Goderich. One of his sons, Captain A. Murray sailed the Great Lakes, captaining the *Frances Smith*, *Spartan* and *Chicora* as well as the *Bayfield* during the first hydrographic survey of the Great Lakes in 1884. Another son, William, became the Dominion Examiner for Masters and Mates at Windsor and Commodore of the Ferry Fleet of the Detroit River. Yet another son drowned in the *Asia* shipwreck.

Cape Croker Chief William McGregor (third from right) at council meeting. William was born of Alexander's marriage to Chief Wahbahdick's daughter.

Alexander's second wife was the daughter of Owen Sound Chief Wahbahdick. Their only son, William, became a chief at Cape Croker First Nation. Eventually Alexander moved to the North Channel where according to family history: ". . . he traded a barrel of whiskey for two young Indian women . . . one became the mother of Duncan McGregor." Descendants of Duncan were respected chiefs of Whitefish River First Nation: Gregor (1918-20); William (1921-32, 1939-54); Augustine (1937-39); and Jim (1970-81).

Alexander McGregor is believed to be buried at the mouth of the Whitefish River.

WHITEFISH RIVER FIRST NATION: BIRCH ISLAND

A Long Legacy

The thirty square mile Reserve No. 4 occupied by the Ojibwe of Whitefish River First Nation is partially demarcated by McGregor Bay, the La Cloche Channel, and Swift Current. Since the signing of the Robinson-Huron Treaty in 1850, the band has lived on the mainland, but retains the name *Wah-Wah-Skin-e-Gah*, Birch Island, as a reminder of the original village site on Old Birch Island (Wardrope Island on boating charts).

Off the southern tip of the reserve lies Great La Cloche Island, which was used as a small camp for fishing and hunting until the Iroquois wars threw the North Shore into turmoil. As part of their campaign to take over the region in the mid-1600s, the Iroquois pushed the Odawa and Ojibwe out of Great La Cloche and established their own settlement. After the Iroquois perished due to a mysterious skin disease, the people of Birch Island returned, and in the late 1700s, were joined by the North West Company which set up a fur trading post.

Places of strong spiritual and cultural significance to the Whitefish River First Nation are scattered throughout the area: Dreamer's Rock, Bell Rocks, Old Birch Island (Wardrope Island) containing old village and burial grounds, and Nehahupkung (Frazer Bay Hill). These sites reveal the community's rich history and its cultural continuity. At the same time, they convey the sometimes devastating effects fur traders, priests, archeologists and governments had on their lives.

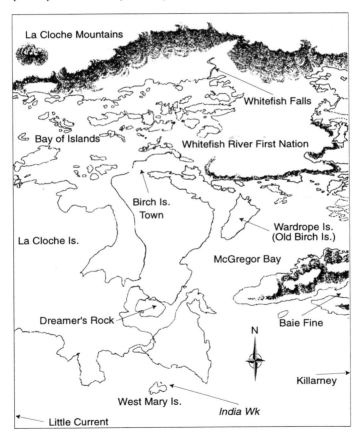

DREAMER'S ROCK AND SHAWONOSWE

Dreamer's Rock is a sacred place, a special gift from the Creator. Towering in gleaming white splendour above the surrounding hills, Dreamer's Rock was an integral part of the traditional rite of passage for Ojibwe youth. Accompanied by an Elder, the pubescent girl or boy would climb to the sacred spot, a depression in the rock in the shape of a human body. After providing a covering and water, the Elder would leave the youngster to begin the spiritual journey.

Several days would be spent in fasting and prayer, during which the youth would receive guidance from a benevolent guardian spirit. Through dreams, the individual hoped to glimpse the future and gain insight into personal strengths and weaknesses.

Of all the youths who began their journeys into adulthood at Dreamer's Rock, there was one boy who stood apart. Spirits did not come quickly to him and despite the teasing of other youth, he increasingly spent more and more time at the sacred place. His name was Shawonoswe, "He-who-faces-the-west." On several occasions when he awakened, he was seen by the Elders to be facing west and because of this they predicted he would become a medicine man. Clearly he had been called to walk the spiritual path, and was destined for greatness.

Shawonoswe grew in stature and power, maturing into a great chief endowed with qualities of leadership and a deep understanding of the mysteries of life. Because of his knowledge of herbs and healing, the sick travelled great distances to consult with him. Through him the Creator imparted laws of governance as well as rules to bring harmony and happiness to the world around them. His people believed he had been entrusted with knowledge of the future and they heeded his visions. Many of his predictions continue to come true. (See Nehahupkung p.11.)

The people of Whitefish River First Nation, descendants of Shawonoswe and his tribe, ask visitors to respect this sacred place and refrain from bringing cameras. As Dreamer's Rock is often in use, the site is only open to the public from 9 a.m. to 4 p.m., Monday to Friday. It is closed on weekends and specified periods of fasting and sweat lodge ceremonies during spring and fall.

WARDROPE ISLAND

Old Birch Island Burial Ground

He arrived at the village of Birch Island in 1938, expressing great interest in the community's heritage and culture. Like the Old Ones he said he believed that the Ojibwe's ancestors had lived in this region long before men migrated to North America across the Bering Strait. As part of his research, he asked to see their traditional sites. Archaeologist Emerson Greenman was then led to the old settlement and graves on Old Birch Island (Wardrope Island). He was shown where the people formerly resided, the large pits that once stored food and the grave sites. The natives knew that for Greenman to examine the past he would have to excavate, but no one thought he would bag, tag and carry off their ancestors to a storage facility in the University of Michigan. Greenman eventually reported his findings. Of one grave he wrote:

> The only definite date is provided by the silver crescent bearing the initials of Robert Cruikshanks, its maker, and this date applied only to grave 18, in which it was found. Cruikshanks was a silversmith who came to Boston from London about 1768, and it is a matter of record that silver ornaments were made by him for the Indians in 1779. . . . Since Old Birch Island lay on the Mackinac-Montreal trade route, it could be expected that trade goods would come to the region soon after their appearance in the eastern centres, and an early date is therefore preferable for Grave 18 and its contents, that is to say, sometime before 1800 and probably as early as 1780. This would mean that the use of the north end [sic west face] of Old Birch Island as a cemetery was known in the area at that time, even though some of the graves may have been made half a century or more before.

Some of the graves dating back to the fur trade were a painful reminder of Ojibwe who had been murdered by a trader after drinking a keg of whiskey laced with poison. Among the earliest casualties of alcohol, these deaths were symbolic of the tragedy wreaked on many native communities as a result of their exposure to this lethal drink. Lands Manager Esther Jacko puts it in historical context, "As alcohol and greed were incorporated into our people through trade, brother turned against brother, tribe against tribe. Combined with this, sickness, disease and poverty created the final divisions which lay the groundwork for the taking of our lands."

Although for Greenman Old Birch Island was just another intriguing research project, for the families of Birch Island the episode was a source of extreme pain. Jacko expresses the community's thoughts: "Who was this person who unearthed our dead and their possessions, then paraded them proudly, inflicting the deepest of wounds from which we have yet to recover, creating in the words of one of our great Chiefs, the end of living and the beginning of survival?"

Instructed by their elders, Whitefish River First Nation has embarked on a healing journey to make reparations to the past. In an effort to have their ancestors' bones returned to Old Birch Island, they contacted the University of Michigan which promised a speedy return if the community would give permission for the extraction of DNA. The Whitefish River band voted against the procedure. At the time of printing, the University has refused to return the bones, citing as justification its mandate to conserve history and culture for all. For the people of Whitefish River First Nation who fought to rescue Nehahupkung and Bell Rocks, this decision is only a temporary setback in their efforts to bring their ancestors home.

BELL ROCK

Voices of the Old and Wisest

It was just a large boulder sitting beside the water. But it was a boulder so wondrous that French *couriers de bois* named the entire region *La Cloche*—the bell.

Assin-mad-wej-wig, "Rock that Sounds" was sacred to the Ojibwe. Countless generations made offerings of tobacco before gently tapping Assin-mad-wej-wig and pressing their ear against the rock. Those whose spiritual ears were open could understand the voices of the spirit world that communicated with them through the rock. To the natives, Bell Rock, among the oldest and wisest of teachers, was placed there to guide and protect them.

They needed this protection when marauding Nadwa-wik (Iroquois) began their drive through Ojibwe lands, killing and plundering and filling the air with terror. Learning of the approach of Iroquois raiding parties, men would strike Assin-mad-wej-wig with heavy stone clubs to awaken the ancestral spirits. It is said their mighty ringing voices resonated as far as forty miles away in Wikwemikong and Sagamok.

One night while the Ojibwe slept, the Iroquois attacked. There had been no time to sound the rock. Carnage ensued. Those fortunate enough to survive returned to honour the dead and buried their loved ones in a common mound sloping gently to the lakeshore. When the wind blew through the trees surrounding the grave, the dead could hear the gentle singing of the pines.

The Iroquois settled all around Assin-mad-wej-wig, yet when they tapped the rock no sound came. The wise one had fallen silent. Then the community fell victim to a terrible skin disease. Even with their great knowledge of medicine, the Iroquois could not cure the illness. Soon they were dead. On their return to Bell Rock, the

Ojibwe carried the bodies of their enemies to a common grave and gave them an honorable burial. They chose a site on a sloping hill near the lakeshore facing east, the direction from which the Iroquois had come.

The years passed until one day, just as their great Chief Shawonoswe had foretold, men with hair on their faces and wearing long robes, arrived and brought dramatic changes. These priests branded the Ojibwe relationship with the rock, idol worship. Although many of the Birch Island people came to accept Christianity, they did not reject their traditional beliefs. For them, there was no conflict between the two. However they kept this view to themselves. Those who continued in the old ways were driven underground and worshipped in secret.

Years later a gravel company working in the area mistakenly cracked Assin-mad-wej-wig so it could fit into the machine to be further ground into gravel. A workman saw the pieces and realized by the peculiar pockmarks that it might be the special Bell Rock that he had heard so much about. He sent word to the village to warn people. Dan McGregor charged to the site and quickly identified the broken pieces of Assin-mad-wej-wig.

The fragments were moved to a place of safe-keeping where they are still revered as symbols of the Ojibwe's once perfect communion with Creation and the Creator. The rock has been silenced, but the Old Ones say that for those who have ears to hear, Assin-mad-wej-wig still holds its promises and echoes messages from the dwelling place of their ancestors.

THE WRECK *INDIA*

What started as an ordinary day for the crew on the 976-ton wooden propeller *India* ended in disaster when flames burst from the boiler. Fire raced through the tinder-dry ship, destroying the lifeboats before they could be launched. Two men on a nearby pulpwood raft pulled up alongside while the crew desperately fled the fire that threatened to engulf the 215-foot vessel. Amid sparks and flames the twelve crew members jumped to safety. As they made their escape, they stared back in shock and disbelief. How could this have happened so quickly?

Even as a wreck, the *India* precipitated another fiery disaster. In 1929 a pleasure yacht struck the wreck and sank. After the yacht was raised, she was towed to a shallow harbour on the north side of West Mary Island and pumped dry. Exploring the dripping interior with lanterns, two men were violently thrown into the air by the force of a blast that rocked the boat. Possibly some hidden gas had been ignited by the lantern flame. The boat disappeared in a billowing fireball. One man was fatally injured, the other seriously burned.

The hulk of the India *rests in 10 to 25 feet of water providing a welcoming habitat for sunfish and perch. Built in 1899, the wooden propeller ship is worth visiting and great for a snorkel on a sunny summer day.*

HEYWOOD ISLAND

An extension of the Niagara Escarpment, the magnificent limestone spine that forms the Bruce Peninsula and demarcates the western shore of Georgian Bay, slips beneath the water and resurfaces as Manitoulin Island before continuing west through northern Michigan. This great dolomite escarpment was laid on top of the Precambrian Shield that makes up the granite basement for the North Channel waters and the shoreline of the North Shore. Heywood Island is remarkable, because the seam of these two opposing rock systems stretches the length of the island. Granite and quartzite, the immutable, metamorphic Shield rocks protrude through the soft malleable sedimentary limestone as the granite cuts its way eastward into Georgian Bay (see Geologically Speaking, p.XI).

The island's protected harbour was once the site of a fishing camp.

WIKWEMIKONG

Manitoulin Island Unceded Indian Reserve
A Community's Fight for Ancestral Land

The Odawa had been pushed off Manitoulin into Michigan and the Lake Superior region by the Iroquois wars in the mid 1600s. Subsequently, in 1833, Father Proulx established a Roman Catholic

Wikwemikong, 1852. Artist is thought to be a nine-year-old boy.

mission. The mission and Indian village of Wikwemikong was, by 1862, not only the oldest permanent settlement on Manitoulin Island but also the largest, boasting over six hundred residents.

In addition to farming, the people of Wikwemikong fished and produced large quantities of maple sugar. In spring it was not unusual to see more than twelve schooners from as far away as Cleveland anchored in Wikwemikong Bay, all eager to make "sweet deals" for the liquid gold—deals that rarely favoured Wikwemikong. Traders commonly charged natives four times market value for their purchases. As one Manitoulin priest observed: "there was a class of whites who attached themselves to the Indian that they might rob him of the fruits of his industry."

Wikwemikong Rejects Treaty

In 1836, the Odawa and Ojibway Nations signed a treaty setting aside the islands along the north shore of Lake Huron and Manitoulin Island for settlement by natives from all over Upper Canada. By 1861, however, much of the good Ontario farmland had been taken, and the government felt compelled to put Manitoulin Island to use. Officials suggested that several small reserves be created for the native populations while the rest of the land would be open to farming.

After a first failed attempt to persuade the natives to give up their island, the job was given to the Superintendent-General of Indian Affairs, William McDougall. McDougall knew his odds were poor. Wikwemikong still opposed the idea and they constituted sixty percent of the population. He implemented a strategy of divide and conquer. First he succeeded in bringing the persuasive Assiginack on side. Then he met with chiefs from the western bands individually. One by one, with the aid of Assiginack, he convinced them to accept the offer of one hundred acres of land per family, with fifty acres for single men. All land-sale moneys—after any surveys were paid—would be placed in a fund for their future use.

By agreeing to the plan, the westerly chiefs, representing approximately forty percent of the Indians, purported to surrender approximately eighty percent of Manitoulin Island. On October 6, 1862, as chiefs of other Manitoulin bands signed, the chiefs and principal men of Wikwemikong stood up and walked away. Outraged Wikwemikong missionaries charged McDougall with

Father Point began a traditional festival featuring horse races and ring games at Wiky, 1848.

gaining acquiescence through liquor, but the deal stood firm. Wikwemikong land, 105,000 acres registered as the Wikwemikong Unceded Indian Reserve, is the only "unceded" reserve in Canada.

Violent Outbreak and an Unsolved Murder

For communities in this unceded reserve (including Wikwemikong, Wikwemikongsing, Chitewaiegunning and Buzwah) the situation was intolerable. Eighty percent of their land had been ceded by a minority of chiefs. They had not signed the treaty and yet they were controlled by its policies and restrictions. Their simmering anger boiled over when white settlers arrived in incident after incident.

First a French Canadian family was forced to vacate

land it had purchased, then two natives who had agreed with the treaty were expelled. The government also began interfering in Indian affairs. It placed restrictions on the sale of Indian firewood, opening up a black-market trade that brought much unwanted liquor into the community. Then it tried to restrict Indians to fishing only in rivers and bays. By the time Commissioner of Fisheries William Gibbard reassigned an Indian fishing ground to a settler named Proulx, the tension was unbearable. Gibbard told the Wiky priest, Father Kohler, to tell the native fisherman of the change. He refused, warning the Commissioner that the citizens of the Unceded Reserve were allied to neither the Canadian nor the British Government and that he had no business meddling. The following day, when the Commissioner saw two boats heading toward the settler, he warned them away at gun point. Following Gibbard's departure from Manitoulin, the Indians forced Proulx off their traditional fishing ground.

When Commissioner Gibbard returned nearly a month later, he was accompanied by twenty-two revolver-wielding constables. According to an article in *The Globe*, July 30, 1863,

> . . . they found about 400 Indians, one of whom was carrying a black flag. They proceeded to the house of the Rev. Jean-Pierre Choné and went inside while the Indians surrounded the house . . . . When they came out Mr. Gibbard ordered the arrest of one of the Chiefs but when the sergeant took hold of the Chief, the other Indians crowded round . . . one rushed forward with uplifted bludgeon and threatened the sergeant's life, but one of

the Toronto specials, Dan Callaghan, placed his pistol at the Indian's head and threatened to pull the trigger.

After the Chief was handcuffed, the priest began to incite the mob to violence. The constables then tried to handcuff the priest. This made the crowd even angrier and the school bell was rung as a signal to attack. Hand to hand combat ensued. Since Gibbard's men were greatly outnumbered, and after Gibbard was told the Indians were prepared to sacrifice their lives for Father Choné, a truce was called. It was agreed the offending parties would go to Quebec to settle their grievances officially.

The tale ends in mystery. Gibbard was last seen in July 1863, returning to Manitoulin on the steamer *Ploughboy*. He never arrived. It was known he was carrying two thousand dollars in treaty payments. Was he robbed and/or murdered? The money was later found in the ship's safe. Nothing was missing except Gibbard's wallet and the porter and bartender. Three days later his body was hauled from the water. Both Father Kohler and Chief Osawanimiki were arrested but no charges were laid.

Wikwemikong Today

Over 3,000 people of Odawa, Ojibwe, and Potawatomi descent live on the Reserve and have made Wikwemikong a vital centre for Indian culture. Each August, dancers, drummers and singers arrive from all across North America to participate in an international pow wow. In addition, the reserve is host to a contemporary native music festival and to the vibrant De-ba-jeh-mu-jig Theatre.

Responding to local needs, the community has also established a health centre that integrates conventional medicine with traditional Aboriginal practices.

MANITOWANING BAY

A Subterranean Passageway

The tagged fish surprised the two fisheries officials. "Where did you say you caught this?" one inquired. "Lake Quanja," the fisherman replied. The officials exchanged glances. The tag identified the large fish as one of hundreds that had been released a few years earlier into Wikwemikong Bay. How on earth did it find its way into an inland lake? Ojibwe spiritual tradition gives an answer: the numerous underground passages that are said to criss-cross Manitoulin Island.

It is said that deep in an underwater cave below Manitowaning Bay (whose name comes from the Ojibwe, *Munidowaning* meaning den of the Manitou) lies the home of Mishebeshu (the Great Lynx). Elders recall two men who tried to measure the depth of this dwelling place by lowering a lead-filled decoy into the bay's dark spot. They never did reach the bottom.

Mishebeshu is lord of the waters and all its creatures. The Ojibwe characterize him as a malevolent underwater monster who manifests himself either in the form of a giant lynx with a spiked tail or a giant serpent. Foaming seas and treacherous waves are created by his thrashing tail and he is said to be responsible when a drowned body is never found. Except in winter when Mishebeshu is under the ice, one must not speak his name aloud in order to avoid his wrath. (For Mishebeshu sightings see Serpent River p.119.)

INDIAN PRESENT GIVING AT MANITOWANING

If Captain Thomas G. Anderson could have seen into the future of Manitoulin's first white settlement, he might have turned back in that spring of 1835. Sent from Coldwater on Georgian Bay, the Indian Agent had but one task on his mind: find a suitable location for the annual gift-giving ceremony. This important gathering, in which elaborate speeches were made and representatives of the British government presented gifts, was intended to strengthen the natives' allegiance to the Mother country, an allegiance which was crucial to the fur trade and in time of war.

His search ended at Manitowaning. It would be ideal: providing plenty of fertile land and a bay deep enough to accommodate a ship laden with presents. Word of the new meeting site spread and the following autumn, Anderson held the first ceremony attended by over 2,500 natives, some travelling five hundred miles to receive the coveted blankets, tobacco, shot, powder, needles, knives, brass kettles and flags.

Describing the scene in *Winter Studies and Summer Rambles in Canada,* travel writer Anna Jameson likened Manitowaning to an amphitheatre filled with wigwams and lodges against a backdrop of hundreds of canoes darting back and forth in the bay; a schooner, "its tall masts furled and half gracefully drooping," silhouetted against the green bank. Over three thousand natives were at this ceremony led by their chiefs, including Potawatomi or "Two Ears," who wore clusters of swan's down hanging from each earlobe, and Wabojeeg, six-foot-four and spectacularly arrayed in scarlet leggings, a colourful belt of wampum and an embroidered headband adorned with four eagle feathers.

Later Jameson attended the chief's assembly,

> The whole number of Chiefs assembled was seventy-five; and take notice that the half of them were smoking . . . When all were assembled . . . Mr. Jarvis rose and addressed them. At the end of every sentence, As-si-ke-nack, (the Black Bird) our chief interpreter here, translated the meaning to the assembly, raising his voice to a high pitch, and speaking with much oral emphasis—the others responding with intervals, "Ha!" but listening in general solemn silence.

Manitowaning during present-giving ceremony, 1845

The interpreter was renowned for once having delivered a speech without pause, from sunrise to sunset. He was more than a man of words however. When necessary he could act forcefully. Hearing that a despised Detroit fur trader was hiding in a cove, Assiginack had boarded the scoundrel's boat and dumped his load of whiskey into the lake. It was to escape this breed of unscrupulous men, who swapped cheap rot gut for gifts then turned around and sold them back to the Indians for valuable furs, that the ceremony had been transferred to Manitoulin from Penetanguishene on Georgian Bay and Amherstburg on the Detroit River.

Following the signing of the 1836 treaty, Captain Anderson anticipated a flood of native settlers. He was determined to make Manitowaning the government centre for all Manitoulin Indians as well as a centre of learning, so he made plans for a school to educate the children and to teach adults trades and farming skills. First he needed white settlers to help build the community and provide teaching services.

An Unsettled Journey:
Manitoulin's First White Settlers

October 1838

Heavy ice weighed down the bateau and huge swells slapped at the gunnels, throwing freezing spray over the thirty-four huddled passengers. Captain Anderson was returning to Manitoulin from Coldwater with his recruits: two oarsmen, a missionary, nurse, schoolmaster, doctor, servants, workers and a few family members including eleven children and six-week-old Benny Bailey. Captain Anderson prayed silently. He had badly miscalculated the number of days required for the journey at this time of year. November with its storms and severe temperatures was fast approaching.

T.G. Anderson in later years

Because it was necessary to make camp early each afternoon in order to feed and bed the children before sunset and because of the time needed to repack and free the boat from the ice each morning, there remained only three or four hours of actual travel time each day. At one point the group became desperately lost in the maze of Georgian

Bay islands. While crossing an island to see if there might be open water at the other side, it seemed Anderson's prayers had been heard. A crow landed nearby and began cawing. Sensing it might be tame, Anderson had everyone follow the bird. Stopping only to let the group catch up, the bird led them to an Indian camp where sympathetic Ojibwe gave them food then piloted them safely through the islands.

Twenty-one days later, suffering from hunger and exposure, the settlers reached Manitowaning, only to be greeted by the sight of one of three residences prepared for them engulfed in flames. All thirty-four had to crowd into two small dwellings. Using sails to partition rooms, they slept fitfully on the floors. The next day, the infant Benny Bailey died from exposure. For days his tiny body lay behind a blanket nailed to the wall, as the family searched for an implement—any implement—to break the frozen ground. Six weeks later a second child joined Benny at the new grave site.

The beleaguered community was dealt yet another severe blow. The schooner laden with their winter provisions was stopped within sight of the island by impenetrable ice. The despairing settlers watched as it sailed away. There was only a small store of provisions and the new community would not have survived without the generosity of local Ojibwe. In addition to teaching the men how to spear fish through the ice, the natives supplied the hungry settlers with maple sugar, partridges, ducks, rabbits, and venison. When a supply ship arrived the following spring, its crew expected to be met by a group of skeletons. What a wonderful surprise to find a healthy, thriving community.

1843: The Establishment Fails, The Town Emerges

Five years later in 1843, Manitowaning had earned the name, The Establishment. The village boasted fifty-five buildings including residences, a store, a mission, stables, and a smithy. Anderson's pleasure at the apparent success of his community gradually turned to disappointment. Within fifteen years only twenty-two buildings remained, and the educational programs had failed. Some blamed the location: Manitowaning Bay lacked fishing grounds. Others pointed to the fact the Ojibwe, having no tradition of farming, resisted permanent settlement. Possibly a more significant factor was the poor response from Upper Canada's native population when invited to migrate to Manitoulin. For the most part, the Indians who did settle on the island came from Lakes Huron and Superior and elsewhere in the United States. Many had allied themselves with the British in the War of 1812 and feared retribution.

The Establishment's death knell came after the Treaty of Manitoulin in 1862. Manitoulin Island reverted to the Crown, which opened it to white settlement. Native communities were moved onto reserves set up according to religious denomination: Catholic, Anglican, and "pagan." When the few remaining Manitowaning natives relocated to the Sheguiandah and Sucker Creek Reserve in 1867, The Establishment seemed destined to fade into oblivion.

With time, however, the village experienced a resurgence thanks to the arrival of new settlers. By 1880, Manitowaning had been transformed by churches, hotels, stores, even a jail. Steamers such as the *Northern Belle*, and the *Jane Miller* called in twice a week.

Today the only reminders of Anderson's Establishment are a few gravestones and St. Paul's, the oldest Anglican Church in northern Ontario, completed in 1848. The 1857 stone jail is now a museum, named after Assiginack, the Odawa orator. On the grounds are a blacksmith shop, a barn, pioneer home and a log schoolhouse. To see the last steam-powered passenger ship on the Great Lakes, visit the S.S. *Norisle*, built in 1946 and operated as a car ferry between Tobermory and Manitoulin Island. The ferry museum, 1883 grist mill, 1885 wooden lighthouse and a restaurant in the former Burn's Wharf Warehouse are all in close proximity to each other.

SHEGUIANDAH

An Ancient Quarry

During a 1951 archaeological survey on Manitoulin Island, Thomas Lee of the National Museum of Canada (now Canadian Museum of Civilization) made one of the most exciting finds of his career. From a high vantage point overlooking Sheguiandah Bay he looked down on ground strewn with quartzite fragments. Seemingly undisturbed, the site extended all the way to the modern village of Sheguiandah.

In three days Lee collected nearly 1,000 artifacts lying on the surface. A later archaeological dig exposed an ancient quarry complete with discarded blades, drills, stone anvil, scrapers and hammer stones. Lee reported the amount of material found at Sheguiandah to be unprecedented in Canada.

The trench, extending down several metres, exposed at least five different levels of occupation defined by changes in tool manufacture. Lee's most controversial discovery was of tool fragments unearthed below sediments deposited after the last period of glaciation. Impossible! Fragments found at that level would place the Sheguiandah quarry nearly 30,000 years ago. This totally contradicted the conventional wisdom that the earliest humans arrived in North America by crossing the Bering Strait during the Ice Age. For many First Nations people however, this merely confirmed a long-held belief that their ancestors had been in this region long before the Ice Age. Needless to say, the theory surrounding the find caused an immense stir throughout the archaeological community. Lee later wrote bitterly in the 1968 article, "Sheguiandah in Retrospect," in the *Michigan Geological Survey*,

> Through four years on the spot geologists studied and debated the evidence . . . The concept of artifacts in and even beneath glacial tills was not easily accepted. Yet every other proposal . . . had to be rejected, after full study. Ultimately, however, the widespread power of conventional belief, stemming from the University of Michigan that an advancing glacier necessarily destroys all traces of man in its path triumphed, and the richest storehouse of Early Man material—and possibly the oldest known in American—fell into neglect, the work stopped, publication blocked, the material hidden away by the National Museum of Canada.

A more recent examination of the site by Dr. Peter Storck of the Royal Ontario Museum together with an expert on glacial lake beaches concluded that the Sheguiandah quarry was positioned on the edge of the former glacial lake Algonquin. What Lee took to be glacial till was actually beach sediment. This places the age of Sheguiandah at about 9,000 B.C. At present little is known about the people who quarried here other than the fact they were hunters and gatherers whose chief source of food would probably have been caribou and mastodon.

SHEGUIANDAH FIRST NATION AND TOWN

When the Anglican Minister Jabez Sims first arrived in 1866, he counted 182 people in 37 families spread out between Little Current, Manitou Lake, Manitowaning and Sheguiandah. At the time there was some question whether the Manitowaning Ojibwe would remain, as the government was delaying a decision on boundaries for native reserves until new settlers had taken up their lands. Tension mounted. Sims accused Charles Latin Dupont, the man entrusted with settling the boundaries, of personally taking land. According to Shelley Pearen's *Exploring Manitoulin*, Dupont called Sims a "brazen faced liar" then punched him in the face. In 1867, Reverend Sims and the Manitowaning group migrated to the native village at Sheguiandah.

Under his guidance, a temporary log church was immediately erected. The present St. Andrews dates from 1886.

St. Andrew's Church built by the Sheguiandah First Nation, 1886

Regrettably, Sims' life was cut short at the age of 39 when he drowned on his way to conduct a christening in Killarney. He is buried close to the reserve in what was once his garden. One of his sons was elected the first mayor of Little Current.

The nearby town of Sheguiandah developed into a prosperous centre anchored by Joseph Walker's grist mill, Ezra Hallman's woollen mill and William Becks' 1879 lumber mill. In 1870, Mr. and Mrs. Dunlop from Pike Lake were hired to make the roof shingles for the grist mill. Over a two-month period they cut 20,000 shingles by hand. For their labours they were paid one bag of flour, one pound of tea and a side of bacon. The mill stood for many years but finally succumbed to progress and was torn down to make way for a highway. The lumber mill survives as the replica Batman Mill, named after James Batman who purchased it around the turn of the century.

In its heyday, Sheguiandah could boast of a brass band and its own literary society, while supporting twenty-seven businesses including the Royal Hotel, a millinary shop, ice cream parlour, the Trotter family cheese factory and a commercial fishery.

STRAWBERRY ISLAND LIGHTHOUSE

A familiar landmark on the North Channel, Strawberry Island Lighthouse was erected in 1881 as part of a string of navigational aids erected along Canada's waterways. One of the earliest lightkeepers was William McKenzie who came to the island in 1883 and stayed until 1919.

In 1984, while on a fishing expedition, Don McKenzie stopped in at the Strawberry Island dock. After exchanging pleasantries with the family leasing the lighthouse, Mackenzie explained he had a personal connection to the island—his father had been born there on April 6, 1883. Because his grandmother's due date had been so close to the opening of the shipping season, she had delivered at the lighthouse. Altogether seven McKenzie children were raised at Strawberry Island.

In those days, before the spring melt, the keeper and his family would cross the ice, their sleigh laden with household goods, some chickens and ducks, a dog and a few cows following behind. Like most small lighthouses with a hand-operated fog horn, its operation involved the whole family. In summer the children polished the lens in the lantern room and tended the cows which had a tendency to roam to the other side of the six-mile island just before milking time. They only attended school from November to March when the family returned to Little Current for the winter.

During Don McKenzie's tour of the lighthouse, he was asked the name of his father. He replied that he was named after his father. The tenant grinned and pointed—on the back door were carved the initials DM.

William and Jane McKenzie with children. Donald, against his father's knees, was born at the lighthouse in April 1883.

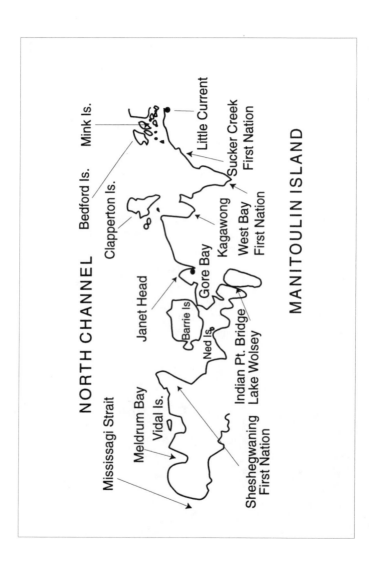

NORTH CHANNEL

Bedford Is.

Mink Is.

Little Current

Sucker Creek
First Nation

Clapperton Is.

Kagawong

West Bay
First Nation

Janet Head

Gore Bay

Barrie Is

Ned Is.

Mississagi Strait

Meldrum Bay

Vidal Is.

Indian Pt. Bridge

Lake Wolsey

Sheshegwaning
First Nation

MANITOULIN ISLAND

2

MANITOULIN ISLAND'S NORTH SHORE

LITTLE CURRENT

Power and Politics: A Dark Lesson

As he watched the smoke belching from the steamer *Collingwood* delivering passengers and supplies to Manitoulin Island, George Abbotossway was struck by an idea. Ships need a reliable source of fuel. The shores of *Wewebjiwang* "where the waters flow back and forth" are covered with forests. Why not set up a wood-fuelling depot here at Little Current?

In the early 1850s, Little Current consisted of six birch-bark wigwams and the wooden shanty Abbotossway and his Caucasian wife, Sarah, called home. The two had met in England (see Sucker Creek p61). As more and more steamers frequented his cordwood pile, George added a store and a native-run fishery. Business was good. What he had not anticipated, however, was a battle with the "Big Trader," the Hudson's Bay Company. The problem began

Geo. Abbotossway's house and stockade 2) Anglican church 3) Mackie's wharves and storehouses 4) small hotel 5) Abrey's store 6) Abrey's residence (old Hudson's Bay Co. store 7) lighthouse and keeper's dwelling (where the waterfront War Memorial now stands)

quite innocently. With government permission the HBC trading post at La Cloche relocated to Little Current and built a store and wharf. Greedily eyeing George's lucrative fuel business, it soon added a fuel depot. Sadly there was not enough traffic to support two enterprises and George's operation began to fail. In 1857, a special commission was sent to Manitoulin to analyse the success of native immigration to the island. Its scathing report highlighted the Hudson's Bay Company's encroachment on Indian land, and described the devastating effects it had had on Abbotossway's business.

The Indian Department agreed with the commission's findings and sent the Hudson's Bay Company packing. However, since the Department had originally approved their move, the HBC felt they should be compensated. When money was slow in coming, the HBC first threatened to remove the dock planking, and then insisted that locals pay for the use of the dock. Later they tried selling the dock to steamship owners. In the end, the Indian Department concluded that the wharf benefitted all Manitoulin Indians and should therefore be purchased from the HBC. Less admirable was the method of payment, outlined in a letter by Reverend James Chance of Garden River:

> it appears that (Indian Agent) Capt. Ironside without any consultation with the Indians made a bargain with the HBC for the wharf, and then went and seized the wood belonging to George Obbotossway to pay for it; wood which George had hired men to cut during the winter and supplied them with provisions whilst cutting it, provisions he had obtained on credit, promising to pay for them as soon as he could dispose of his wood this summer. I think you will agree with me in saying that a more arbitrary, unjust and tyrannical act on the part of Captain Ironside could not possibly have been perpetrated.

Complaints from Abbotossway and others reinforced this charge but fell on deaf ears. In a patronising letter, the Indian Department backed their Manitoulin Agents: ". . . the Governor General is very glad to hear that they [the Indians] are all so industrious, and trying to support their families, but he wishes them to remember that the wood they cut does not belong to them alone, but to all the Indians on the Island." No mention was made of Abbotossway's losses.

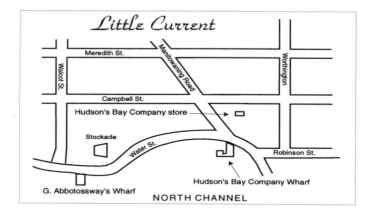

Little Current Becomes A Town

George Abbotossway's instincts about Little Current's superb location were correct. By the 1870s it was considered Manitoulin's premiere port. Steamers such as the *Northern Belle, Iroquois, Ploughboy* and the *Asia* delivered supplies, furniture and settlers, then loaded on cattle and produce destined for eastern markets.

Since competition between the steamship lines often reached absurd proportions, the wharves were sure to provide entertainment. James Barry's *Georgian Bay: The Sixth Great Lake* reported from an 1892 Manitoulin newspaper,

> Capt. Pete Campbell of the *Pacific* came in Wednesday with three niggers [winches] and a Sheguiandah cheese on the safety valve and the keel carefully greased to prevent friction. The story they brought was that they had beaten the *City of*

Midland by five minutes and 37.12076 seconds between Collingwood and Owen Sound. You could see the Cap's smile half way to Strawberry [Island] shining like the church steeple and his chin whisker was sticking out at an angle of 90 degrees with excitement.

The article went on to report that the *City of Midland* pulled in later, and quickly tended to its business before "Capt. Bassett once more started on the trail of the *Pacific* with blood in his eye. All the paint was burnt off her smokestack." Who needed horse racing?

Despite the steamer service, Little Current was limited by the fact that it was situated on an island. A railway bridge linking Manitoulin to the North Shore was a necessity. For decades politicians dangled empty promises before the residents. During one election campaign, a barge-load of rails was dumped on Goat Island where it was allowed to rust

Little Current's waterfront, 1902

Water Street, 1902

until just before the next election when a few feet of track were laid. When resident Mrs. Turner was asked to drive in the first spike, she coolly replied she would prefer to hammer in the last. Finally, in 1913, a swing bridge was completed. Hopes for a new era of prosperity were high.

While the bridge and train made life easier for the islanders, it was not the only item on their transportation wish list. The newly-invented car was all the rage. However, since the bridge was built to accommodate trains only, off-island travel was impossible. Even if cars made it to the mainland, there was no connecting road on the North Shore. It was not until 1929 that the highway from Espanola reached the North Shore and Manitoulin residents received a ferry service. This continued until 1945 when the old swing bridge was modified to permit car traffic.

Wewebjiwang, "where the waters flow back and forth," is a much more accurate description than the name Little

Current. In fact, Little Current is a misnomer, suggesting nothing of the unpredictability of the powerful current which often flip-flopped from east to west wreaking havoc for tugs hauling log booms through the narrow channel between Little Current and Goat Island. Since 1885, attempts had been made to slow the current through dredging and dynamiting (Magazine Point on Goat Island gained its name from the dynamite stored at the site) but they were never completely successful. One of the worst situations arose in 1906 when an adverse current caused two booms, each containing 100,000 logs, to hem in steamers at the dock for five days. While captains whined about lost revenues, crews held an impromptu baseball game.

Several years later, train service was stopped for three days because the swing bridge could not be closed. The current had pinned a freighter up against the bridge's cement abutment. Following the introduction of rail service in 1913 a coal facility sprang up on Goat Island. Coal from West Virginia and Ohio was delivered by boat, then loaded onto Algoma Eastern Railway trains heading for Sudbury, North Bay and Cochrane. By 1930, this depot was the town's chief source of employment since the lumber mills had shut down and shipping traffic had slowed to a trickle. Old-timers recall how men with their paper bag lunches waited on the dock in hopes of getting twelve hours of work shovelling coal into the ships' holds. Little Current resident Norman Smith recalls, "It was a messy business, soft coal. I can remember the women wouldn't hang their laundry—they'd say 'Oh I can't wash today; the wind is blowing from the east or from the north because of the coal dust.' They'd curse that."

J & T Conlon's mill on Picnic Island surrounded by lumber.

But like the wood-fuelling depots and the lumber mills, coal too had its day. Norman Smith recalls the first diesel train to arrive on Goat Island, "When I started at the CPR in 1950 I worked on steam engines . . . then all at once they said 'we've got trains that burn oil—no more coal.' People didn't realize the impact it would have." In 1965 the coal hoist stopped operating, and it was dismantled in 1966.

Tourism is at the heart of the town today with yachts and cruisers replacing steamers and schooners along the wharves. A small museum housed in the old telephone switchboard facilities on the second floor of Turner's of Little Current opens a window onto the past. At nearby Picnic Island, the crumbling cathedral-like ruins of J. & T. Conlon's mill stand as a reminder of the days when Little Current was known as "Sawdust Town." Further evidence of these long-gone mills are still turning up, such as the dozens of twenty-foot laths found at the bottom of the lake between Spider and Low Islands.

THE *HIAWATHA* SHIPWRECK

Before a bridge was built linking Manitoulin Island to the North Shore, a trip to Sudbury or to the Sault was a major undertaking. Horses and buggies or Model Ts would battle Manitoulin's notoriously bad roads to Gore Bay, where travellers would board the mail boat to the North Shore. The last leg of their journey was completed by train.

On completion of the highway between Espanola and the North Shore in 1929, the *Hiawatha*, a twelve-car ferry was brought into service. Prices were set at 75 cents per car and 20 cents per passenger. Built in 1874 as a ferry between Dresden and Sarnia, the *Hiawatha* suffered a fire in 1887, a grounding in 1906, and retirement in 1924. She was reactivated to serve the Manitoulin community between 1930-31, before retiring permanently. After moving to her current location on the northeastern shore of Low Island, the *Hiawatha* burned to the waterline. Her remains lie between 5-30 ft. (1.5-9 m) underwater but are difficult to see because of silt stirred up by heavy boat traffic. A wreck symbol marks the location on the chart. Just east of the swing bridge there is another wreck marked on the charts which, if the light is right, can be seen from the surface. According to Cris Kohl's *Dive Ontario*, it was a small wooden steamer called the *Alexandra*.

EDWARD BUCKLEY WRECK

The lumber trade was booming. For Michigan businessman Ed Buckley sales were up and his company had just commissioned a new steamer to be named after him. On September 1, 1929, only a year after Buckley's death, the boat burned southeast of Mink Island and sank in over a hundred feet of water. The 155-ft. (46.3m) steamer waited in the cold dark waters for nearly sixty years before she was discovered by a diver from Little Current. According to Cris Kohl's *Dive Ontario Two*, the wreck is sitting upright in 110 ft. (33m) with her anchor chain leading down to the main part of the hull. This is a dark, cold, silty site not recommended for any but advanced divers.

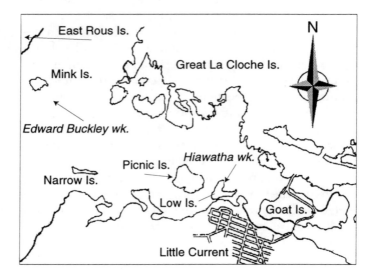

EAST AND WEST ROUS

Old-timers tell the story of desperate locals, during the Great Depression, who started fires on the Rous Islands in hopes of being hired as fire fighters.

BEDFORD ISLAND

The Bootlegger of Cut-Knife Cove

Around 1919, a German brother and sister called the Schraeders lived in a homestead above Cut-knife Cove. They tended their small farm and garden, and Mr. Schraeder, in peaked cap and brass-buttoned jacket, busied himself with woodwork and supplying his excellent hooch to the locals. He did not have far to go to find customers. A shingle mill operated on Strange Bay and there were a number of lumber camps in Wise Cove.

One day, the long arm of the law stretched to the Bedford farm, but Schraeder was well prepared. He had stored his brew under the floorboards. As the police tore through the house, marching back and forth over the contraband, Schraeder tried hard to suppress a grin.

SUCKER CREEK FIRST NATION

Sucker Creek's history begins long ago with the Abbotossway family. Wishing to remain loyal to Britain, the Abbotossways left Mackinac Island shortly after the American Revolution and eventually relocated on Manitoulin Island.

Native farms were run much like co-operatives.

George, a second generation Abbotossway living on Manitoulin, was sent to England in 1838 to learn English. Here he met and fell in love with Sarah Newman who immigrated to Canada and worked as a maid for Reverend O'Meara on Manitoulin to pay for her passage. The two married and settled in Little Current (see Little Current p.51). After the 1862 treaty Abbotossway and other native families, many of whom fished and cut wood for him, were given a shock; they were to be forced to move. Several reserves had been created around old villages (such as Wikwemikong) but the people living in Little Current were not so fortunate; Little Current's harbour was going to be needed for the anticipated rush of non-native settlers.

Their new home, Sucker Creek, was likely chosen for its harbour but the new citizens were never thrilled with the swampland that went along with it. Nevertheless they became successful farmers, running their farms like co-operatives where farmers exchanged surplus crops so that everyone enjoyed a diverse food supply.

George Abbotossway became the first Hereditary Chief of Sucker Creek First Nation and was followed by his son, Charles, who held the position for 45 years. One of his other sons, Tom, joined Buffalo Bill's Wild West Show.

The name "Potossway" is common on Mackinac Island, and Corella Abbotossway Corbiere believes that the Potossways are likely related to her ancestors since many native surnames were misspelled phonetically by government officials. Recently the Abbotossways learned of another interesting connection. During the Riel Rebellion in 1885, several Abbotossways (then spelled Obbotossway) went to Manitoba to help the Métis. Because they never returned it was assumed they were killed in battle. However, in the last few years, Obbotossways from the west have returned to claim their ancestral roots.

WEST BAY FIRST NATION

Around 1848, Father Hanipaux counted 96 Ojibwe and Odawa living at what they called *M'Chigeeng*, "stepping stones of the cliffs," (West Bay). Two years earlier these families, who had originally immigrated from Wisconsin, separated from Wikwemikong.

The government first attempted to open Manitoulin

Island to European settlement in 1861. This would involve rescinding the Treaty of 1836 which set aside Manitoulin Island for settlement by native peoples only. In February of that year, all the males on Manitoulin gathered at Wikwemikong. Meetings had already been held at Sheshegwaning, and West Bay and these communities were in solidarity: they would not give away their island. The tension in the air was palpable. All but two chiefs agreed. One man spoke: "Any one of our chiefs who would refuse to unite with us in the defense of our rights should no longer be considered as our chief. Let all those who think like me raise their hand." The dissenting chiefs were removed and Kinojameg Jr., Wakegijik, and Ominakamigo were elected in their place, with a mandate to oppose the new treaty. The next year, 1862, the government used a new strategy with the chiefs, producing very different results (see Wikwemikong p.31).

By the 1890s, West Bay First Nation, the second largest reserve on the island, had over three hundred residents. To earn a living they fished, farmed, logged, loaded freight (for a dollar a day), and produced over 10,000 pounds of maple syrup each year. At the school, an extensive garden was planted to teach the children agricultural techniques. In 1972, following the destruction of the original church, a new one was built in the shape of a teepee. Inside, traditional elements of native culture were incorporated into the decor. West Bay has set up an Ojibwe cultural foundation for those interested in learning more about First Nation history, and each July, the community hosts a pow-wow.

CLAPPERTON ISLAND

The Longest Lightkeeping Family on the Canadian Great Lakes

The story of Clapperton light is the story of the Baker family, faithful lightkeepers over a period of 88 years between 1875-1962. Their legacy began with Benjamin Baker, Clapperton's second lightkeeper, whose duties ended with his mysterious disappearance in 1894 (see Benjamin Islands p.97) and continued with his son Henry, who died from complications following an accident while tending the range lights at Cartwright Point.

For years, Henry had complained to the Department that the lights should be moved back from the shore, away from the icy spray that made the cables brittle. He was ignored because freighter captains contended that moving the lights would force them closer to Clappertons's shore

Clapperton Island lighthouse

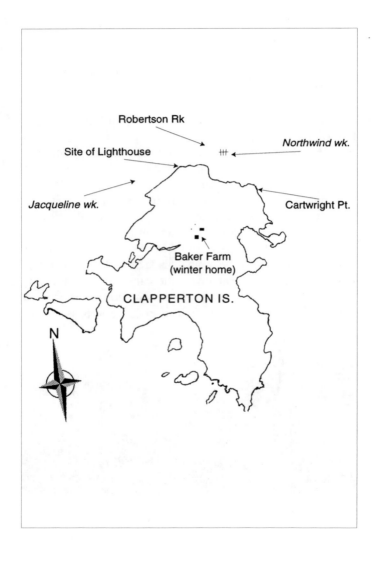

and nearer to treacherous Robertson Rock. It took Henry's accident to change their minds. The cable did break and the falling lantern crushed his shoulder and broke his ribs.

Misfortune also dogged Henry's son William. He was alone on the island when his appendix ruptured. He became delirious, collapsing as he tried to drag himself to replenish the lighthouse oil that had run out. Fortunately, William was found and taken to the hospital by two men from Kagawong. His nephew, Norm Lloyd, rushed over to the island to tend the light temporarily.

Today, the only evidence of the Bakers' long residence on the island is their nineteenth-century log house and barn in the island's interior. The Clapperton lighthouse was rolled down the rocks and towed to Spanish, where it stuck on a sandbar and sat for a considerable time until the water level dropped enough for it to be retrieved. A metal beacon now sits on its former site.

NORTHWIND WRECK

It is a thrill to swim through the dark waters of the North Channel and suddenly coming across this huge 2,476-ton freighter, especially when you see the name on the side of the ship. The *Northwind* was a 300-ft. (89.9m) steel freighter built in 1888. On July 1, 1926, she hit Robertson rock and within two hours sank to the bottom. The wheelhouse blew off as the water filled her hull, but no lives were lost. The ship now sits intact and upright in over a hundred feet of water. Anchors, portholes and the four-blade propeller are all visible. This is a very deep site and much caution must be taken. Do not try to penetrate the hull! To find the site, look east of Robertson Rock for a float that is usually placed on the wreck by a dive club from Sudbury.

In the same area, try looking for the *Jacqueline*, a double-ended car ferry which sank in 1887. The wreckage is scattered around the north tip of Clapperton Island in 5-10 ft. (1.5-3m) of water.

KAGAWONG

Tragic Death of the Town's Founders

In 1873, the brothers Robert and William Henry were offered eight hundred acres of virgin timber if they would augment their plans for a lumber mill at Bridal Veil Falls with a grist mill and the settlement of twelve families at Kagawong. They not only fulfilled these obligations but they also donated lumber to construct a boarding house, dock, store, school and St. Paul's Church.

For nine years, the brothers' enterprising spirit imbued Kagawong which means "where mists rise from the falling waters," with energetic confidence. But in 1882 this was all snatched away. The first blow was Robert Henry's death after a fire on the steamer *Manitoulin*. Started from an overturned coal-oil lamp, the fire quickly turned the ship into a floating inferno. As the Captain rammed her aground, passengers jumped screaming from the ship while others clambered down ropes into the frigid water.

Eleven perished, and many were injured. After heroically rescuing several passengers Robert Henry survived, only to suffer a fatal heart attack soon after. The entire town filled St. Paul's for his memorial service. Five months later there was a second service, this time for William, one of over 120 people drowned when the steamer *Asia* vanished in a hurricane. The *Asia* was the largest Canadian marine disaster of the time.

But Kagawong was blessed. The Henrys' mill and other holdings were purchased in 1896 by James Carter, a man as civic-minded as his predecessors. He built the Billings Company store, beautified the town by adding sidewalks and constructed steps at Bridal Veil Falls, a favoured picnic place.

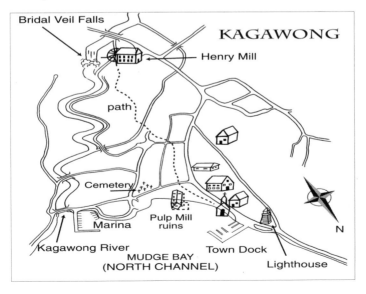

Stacked wet pulp beside the mill was transported on rail cars to loading docks and used in the manufacture of catalogues.

Thanks to the more than twenty-four lumber mills operating in the area, Kagawong grew into a town of two hundred people. The harbour was alive with commercial fishing, boat-building and the noise of penned livestock awaiting shipment.

Nevertheless, this was not enough for the entrepreneurial James Carter. He offered complimentary use of his water power (provided by the Falls) to any company willing to relocate to Kagawong. In 1925 the Little Rapids Pulp Company of Wisconsin accepted and Manitoulin gained its first and only pulp mill. The site chosen by the company happened to be where Oliver Berry's residence and boat-building operation stood. Berry agreed to move and it was quite a sight to see thirty horses straining for two days to haul the house up the hill.

At the same time as the pulp mill was under construction, a canal was dug from the Kagawong River to a five-foot-high wooden pipe which diverted water to the mill site. Each day twenty tons of wet pulp was produced and transported by rail car out on a long pier in Mudge Bay. From there it was shipped to Kalamazoo, Michigan where it was processed into paper for Sears-Roebuck catalogues. The mill's limestone structure remains an impressive sight on the shores of Mudge Bay.

Today, much of Kagawong's original architecture still stands as a reminder of this once-bustling north shore town. A local tour map of historic sites directs the visitor to picnic sites at the former Henry/Carter mill location and the lovely Bridal Veil Falls. There is a pleasant nature trail that leads from the town to the falls.

THE TUG *EVERETT*

To the east of the mill along the shore you can see the large boiler of the fishing tug *Everett*. Built in 1900, the 56-ft. (16.8m) vessel was owned by the Graham Brothers fishery and was a familiar site along the north shore of Manitoulin until it was abandoned in the 1940s. The rest of the boat lies scattered in the bay in less than 10 ft. (3m) of water and can be seen from the surface.

GORE BAY

A Spirited Pioneer Town

No one knows which is the true origin of Gore Bay's name: the gore-shaped inner bay at Little Point, or the steamer *Gore*, forced to winter over in the early 1800s.

Long before European settlers appeared, a large Ojibwe settlement sat at the south end of the present town. When the first homesteaders arrived around 1869, the future town site was thickly covered with cedar forests laced with old Indian trails.

The region's rich soil proved ideal for farming and the sheltered bay quickly attracted entrepreneurs. By 1880, when the grist and lumber mills were working at peak levels, a massive holding pond for logs filled the bay and piles of milled lumber covered the shore where the government dock now stands. One of the many characters who added colour to the town was Dave Bickell, owner of a shingle mill. While demonstrating with great flourish how he accidentally cut off one finger, he unwittingly removed another. Old-timers laughingly remember Bickell's technique for convincing local customers to buy his shingles: he would hold up a shingle together with his stubbed hand and declare proudly, "Our own make!"

In spring and fall, packet steamers such as the Northern Navigation Company's *Midland, Pacific, Atlantic*, and *Germanic* delivered supplies to the permanent residents and in summer brought tourists to fill the village's three hotels.

Gore Bay looking south, 1905.

One evening, the *Caribou* pulled into port many hours behind schedule. Freight was unloaded on the port side, and then the steamer switched docks to load cattle on the starboard side. The animals ambled up the gangplank, across the deck, and out the gangway on the other side, left open by an absentminded crew member. Chaos ensued as cattle were chased by men in rowboats. On shore the cattle fanned out and ran amuck through streets and gardens, bringing exasperation mixed with laughter to the frantic rescuers.

Near the turn of the century, Gore Bay was given the nickname "Tin Horn town" in honour of its brass band. Small businesses thrived, including four shoemakers who were kept busy hand-sewing fine footwear for the townspeople and knee-high boots for the farmers. The biggest sellers were spike-soled boots for the unemployed farmers, mill and dock workers heading to the lumber camps in winter.

When Gore Bay was chosen to be the judicial seat for the new District of Manitoulin, a courthouse and registry office were built in 1889. Today Gore Bay's genteel old houses and tree-lined streets testify to the town's early prosperity. In the Western Manitoulin Historical Society Museum, housed in the 1879 jail, fascinating artifacts, antiques and photographs recreate the flavour of Manitoulin's pioneer experience.

JANET HEAD LIGHTHOUSE

Death and Scandal

The logbooks written by Janet Head's first keeper, Robert Boyter, have been preserved. They are filled with detailed accounts of supplies, boat traffic, trivial incidents, even the odd complaint and they are testament to the amount of work and the tedium faced by lightkeepers and their families. One of Boyter's accounts, however, is "of a very melancholy nature." He tells of the tragic death of his wife and the crippling of his son when the two were caught in bad winter weather, attempting to cross over to the North Shore.

Boyter, a Mr. Thorne and a Mr. Lewis, and two young girls set out to retrieve them, but they too became trapped by another storm. The horses refused to proceed, and so the group huddled in the sleigh under bed ticks and buffalo blankets through one night and into the next before Boyter and Thorne left the party to find help. In the morning, they thankfully met up with a search party. By the time the ordeal was over, Mr. Lewis' feet had to be amputated, and one of the girls had died. There was talk of alcohol having been involved, of Boyter and Thorne having sheltered themselves at the expense of the others. An air of suspicion swirled around the horrifying event, and rocked the community for years.

CAMPBELL BAY AND LAKE WOLSEY

Indian Point Bridge: The Amazing Pike Story

Sometime around 1900, the causeway and bridge dividing Lake Wolsey and Campbell Bay was built. Manufactured by the Hamilton Bridge Company, the bridge sections were shipped to Manitoulin and assembled on site. Workers on the causeway would heat rivets to red-hot perfection then toss them to the bridge where crews hammered them into place.

For years, Campbell Bay and Lake Wolsey had been known for their northern pike. A boy heading home with a 35-lb. pike sagging over his shoulder, its tail dragging on the ground, was not an unusual sight. One day a bridge worker watched as a rivet missed its intended landing spot and tumbled toward the lake. No sooner did it strike the water than a big pike leapt up. Immediately the worker raced to shore and madly rowed to the place he had last spotted the fish. That day for lunch he served a grilled 15-lb. pike—absolutely delicious despite the hole burned in its belly.

BARRIE ISLAND

Despite its name, Barrie Island is connected to Manitoulin by a narrow neck of land. Originally covered with lush stands of maple, ash and birch, its rich soil encouraged settlers to clear the land for farming.

For a brief period around 1900, having secured contracts to grow sugar beets for a refinery in Wiarton, the farmers harboured dreams of cash bonanzas. In the fall they arrived at the proposed shipping site, their wagons piled high with beets, only to be met with the devastating news that the sugar refinery had gone bankrupt. (The financially troubled plant had been dealt a death blow when a worker opened the wrong valve allowing all the beet pulp to spew into Georgian Bay.) A measure of fame and fortune did come to Barrie Island thanks to the vile-tasting but mineral rich waters of Mervyn Creek. Hordes of health-conscious tourists flocked to the "Island," all hoping for a magic cure.

THE HERMIT OF NED ISLAND

Ned Island was named after the somewhat eccentric Ned (Edwin) Saunders, one of the first residents of Gore Bay. Sometime after his arrival in 1869, he decided to move to an earthen cave-like dwelling built along the shore. Over the years, he was forced to move several times in order to keep his distance from encroaching settlers. A former scholar who enjoyed books and loved music (rumour hait he played a church organ in England), Ned

Ned's famous brother Sir Charles Saunders—a plant breeder who developed Marquis wheat, revolutionizing yields.

was content with a simple life. He grew vegetables and traded fish for bread and other supplies. Despite his reclusive nature, he was known for his humour, military posture and love of walks . . . long walks. It is said he once walked from Owen Sound to London, Ontario, a distance of 140 kms.

SHESHEGWANING FIRST NATION

Sheshegwaning is one of the oldest communities on Manitoulin. According to the band, *Sheshegwaning* means "where there are rattlesnakes." When local students researched the history of Sheshegwaning, they learned that elders attributed the name to rattlesnakes from a nearby island (likely Vidal Island, see below). At one time the Indian village had been on the banks of Vidal Bay. The Odawa settlement of Sheshegwaning was an industrious, close-knit community of trappers and fishermen, craftsmen and boat builders, loggers and farmers. Together the residents built a Roman Catholic church and school and shared their skills and resources with all who lived there.

VIDAL ISLAND'S LEGENDARY RATTLESNAKES

In 1933, a zoologist at the Royal Ontario Museum received a package containing the tail of an exceptionally large massasauga rattlesnake with six full-grown pairs of rattles and a seventh sprouting. The snake had been caught by Bert Witty on Vidal Island, which was better known, for obvious reasons, as Rattlesnake Island.

The story of how the snakes came to inhabit the island is part of native oral tradition. Long ago a trading ship grounded just off the island. An Indian was hired by the traders to protect the cargo while they sought help. During their absence, nearby natives distracted the lone guard and looted the ship. The enraged traders decided to solicit help from a respected medicine man. After a generous payment, the medicine man issued a warning to the culprits—return the cargo or suffer a plague of rattlesnakes. No one took him seriously until snakes began to appear on every rock and crevice. Almost immediately, as if by magic, the loot appeared. The snakes, however, stayed.

Meldrum Bay

It was a homesick water surveyor who named Meldrum Bay for a market town in his native Scotland. Fourteen years later, in 1876, homesteaders began purchasing lots in the newly-created Dawson Township and the name Meldrum Bay was added to the list of ports of call along Manitoulin's shores. Unlike some of the other villages—Little Current, Gore Bay, Kagawong—which were carved out of lush, virgin forest, Meldrum Bay was dubbed "Burnt Land" because of its landscape charred by a forest fire. Yet while the site lacked aesthetic appeal, it was a welcome sight to the farmers who had to clear the land.

The area was plagued by subsequent fires, including two in 1910. Such a pall of thick smoke hung over the region that Meldrum Bay fishermen had to hang cowbells on the buoys in order to find their nets. At Mississagi Strait lighthouse, keeper Jim Ball, fearing ships might founder on the shoals, kept the steam-powered fog horn blowing for so many days he ran out of coal.

The second fire started aboard the tug *Winslow* while it was docked. One crew member was badly burned trying to escape. To protect the dock and the 1,000,000 board feet of lumber awaiting shipment, the *Winslow* was towed out but sank not far from the dock, creating a dangerous hazard for boats heading in and out of the bay. After years of complaints, the government paid to have it removed in the 1930s.

A 1910 forest fire put such a cloak of haze over Meldrum Bay and region, the Mississagi Strait lighthouse keeper sounded the foghorn for days, running out of coal.

In 1880, storekeeper William Switzer built the first sawmill, and found himself being undercut by the shipping industry. Many a Meldrum Bay barn was constructed, not out of lumber from his mill but from lumber found strewn along the shore. (During a storm, barges frequently lost cargo from their decks.) In 1901, the Manitoulin Ranch and Lumber Company took over the Switzer mill and expanded production to include shingles and laths. With only one mill and only one bar at the Meldrum Bay Inn, the town was spared the rowdiness that characterized other mill towns such as Blind River. The closure of the company in 1914 precipitated a dramatic exodus from town. But seizing the opportunity, Archie Wickett opened a sawmill in 1919 to meet the demand for fish-packing boxes. By the 1930s he was doing such a booming trade the harbour was renamed Fish Box Bay.

The advent of steamships marked the end of the sailing era but the odd tired schooner still called in occasionally. In a 1956 *Manitoulin Expositor* article, Archie Wickett recalled the laborious process of lifting hardwood ties over the rails of the schooner *Azov* in 1911. The *Azov's* hard-driving Captain Red MacDonald had a unique crew for that time, his two daughters (who no doubt had little say in their career choice). Leaving Meldrum Bay, one daughter would be at the helm, the other handling the rigging. When news arrived that the *Azov* had foundered en route to Saginaw Bay with her full complement of hardwood ties and pilings from Gore Bay, everyone was shocked. But no one was shocked to hear that the Captain had insisted the crew row all night to Goderich instead of landing on the much closer Michigan shore.

For most residents, life was hard. A fisherman's day began before dawn at the dock, and continued until long after dark when they packed their fish and prepared for the next day. As in other Manitoulin communities, Meldrum Bay's farmers and mill hands turned into lumberjacks over the winter. Long-time resident Melvin Trick recalls his father was still working seasonally as a lumberjack when he died at the age of seventy from a heart attack.

A highlight of any visit to Meldrum Bay is the Net Shed Museum, built in 1907 by Trick's father-in-law, Joseph Millman, and his partner Jack Keen. It houses fishing, logging and pioneer artifacts along with other local memorabilia such as the World War II camp kit belonging to Millman's daughter Edna who served as a nurse overseas in the Canadian Army.

WINSLOW WRECK

Learning to Dive the Hard Way

In 1934, Jimmy McColman's new dive suit cost him a stiff $2,000, complete with bronze hard-hat as heavy as a boulder, thick waterproof canvas suit, gloves, weights, lead-soled boots, a hand-operated oxygen pump and an oxygen line. However it was worth the price if he and his two sons could ride out the Depression by salvaging steel from shipwrecks. Their first job was to remove the *Winslow* wreck that was obstructing the Meldrum Bay dock.

The McColmans had a job, the right equipment but there was one problem: no instructions about how the new-fangled suit worked. After a lot of discussion, they agreed that son Ken would dive, Mr. McColman would operate the hand pump to supply the oxygen and they both would hope for the best.

Fully-suited, Ken jumped into the water. But instead of sinking, he floated like a balloon. Mr. McColman pulled him back to the boat and wrapped enough chain around the suit until Ken sank. Drifting downward, he was suddenly overcome by nausea and frantically tugged the line. In only moments he was at the surface and tore off the helmet. "Oh I heaved up everything I'd eaten in the last six months," recalls Ken. "I went down again and they had to pull me up again. I said, 'I just can't go down in that suit—there's something wrong!' 'Oh you little puffer,' my

The McColmans ready to blow up the shipwreck Winslow. *R to l: Ken McColman; (father) Jim McColman; Wilfred Williams; Doug Steele; Alex McColman; and Arden Bailey*

old man said, 'you never want to do anything.' Oh he was a tough character."

Impatient with his son's unwillingness to continue, Mr. McColman suited up. Weighed down by a full length of chain, he sank—and promptly signalled to be brought back to the surface. "We pulled him out, took the helmet off, and he vomited up everything. He was in bed for five days after it. While he was in bed my brother and I operated on the suit to find what the hell was wrong with it."

The boys discovered that the spring in the relief valve was too stiff. They were getting oxygen but the suit was not expelling the carbon dioxide they breathed out. They were being poisoned. After removing a number of coils in the spring, the suit was ready to go. (The spring lasted until they retired the suit in 1957.)

Before returning to the *Winslow*, the McColmans waited until the harbour was frozen in order to protect the town from the explosions. It took Ken five weeks working below the ice eight hours a day in complete darkness to lay the 64 boxes of dynamite needed to blow up the ship. When they finally detonated the *Winslow*, the shock wave blew out a window or two in town. The McColman's salvaging career spanned twenty years and included an estimated 107 wrecks and enough close calls—like being sucked up into the water intake pipe of the Blind River mill—for Ken to earn the nickname, "Nine Lives."

LAURA H. LEE AND *ALBERTA M. WRECKS*

The Meldrum Bay waters are a treasure chest for snorkelers and divers: pilings from the old wharf, dock cribs and two wrecks. The *Laura H. Lee*, a small tug that sank in 1929 is located south of the public dock and north of Macrae Cove. The boat was riding out a late November gale when a kerosene lamp was knocked over . . . you can imagine the rest. Not much remains of the vessel but the wooden rudder is interesting.

Across the bay from the public docks, on the east side of Welsh Island, are the remains of the *Alberta M*. This 1907 steam fishing tug was operational until the spring of 1946 when it ran aground. It lies in only three feet of water just south of the cabin and is easily viewed from a canoe. (Yes, those really are ribs of the hull despite looking like remains of a makeshift dock.) The island is privately owned.

MISSISSAGI STRAIT LIGHTHOUSE

Skull proof of La Salle's Griffon?

Searching for a suitable tree to make a new sailboat mast, lightkeeper William Cullis (1877-1900) and assistant John Holdsworth made their way through the forest.

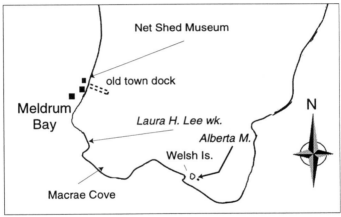

Suddenly Holdsworth spotted a rabbit. With thoughts of a delicious stew in mind he tracked the animal along a bluff until he reached a small cave. Entering, his heart stopped. There were four skeletons slumped against the wall. Could these be connected with the mysterious shipwreck on the beach which some claimed to be La Salle's ship, the *Griffon*? One skeleton in particular sparked his curiosity. He picked up a jaw bone and held it against his own face. It fit completely around. Holdsworth backed away stunned. La Salle's pilot had been nicknamed "Luc the Dane" and was reputed to have been a towering seven feet tall. Could this be his?

The *Griffon* had had a short career. Having gained official sanction to follow the Mississippi River to its mouth and to set up a string of fur-trading forts along the way, René-Robert Cavelier Sieur de La Salle had commissioned a barque to be built at Niagara Falls in 1678. By September 1679, he was in Green Bay, Lake Michigan with the *Griffon* full of furs. Chronically in debt, La Salle ordered the cargo to be taken back to Niagara in order to pay off the expedition's financial backers. The *Griffon* sailed with a crew of five under Luc the Dane and was never seen again.

The wreck on the lighthouse beach had been known to local Indians long before the lighthouse was built in 1873. Over the years its resources were plundered. During World War I, the lead used to caulk the ship's planking was pried out and melted down by fishermen to make net sinkers, while farmers used the iron bolts to make harrow teeth. In the 1920s, boys set fire to the wreck in order to salvage the rest of the iron. After this recycling whatever scraps survived were swept back into the Strait during a storm. And there the answer to the *Griffon* mystery still lies.

As for the skeletons, most of the bones were lost but the skulls sat lined up along the boathouse dock until someone kicked them into the water. Near the cave, Holdsworth had found several buttons and coins and for years they sat in a baking powder can in the fog plant until they too were misplaced.

Today the Mississagi Lighthouse is a repository of *Griffon* lore as well as a museum honouring the five keepers who worked the light from 1873 until its automation in 1968. Displays include old photographs, furniture and paraphernalia from the lighthouse days.

La Salle's Griffon *vanished with crew and cargo, 1679*

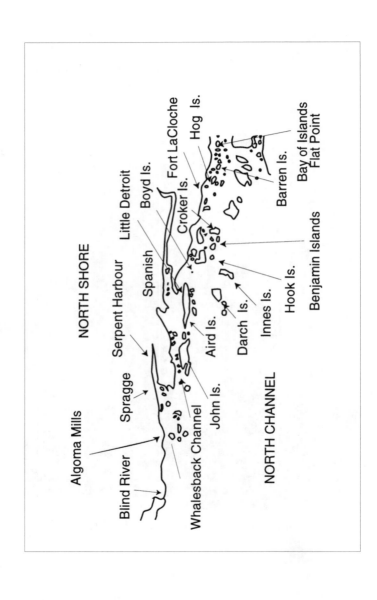

3

BAY OF ISLANDS TO BLIND RIVER

BAY OF ISLANDS/FLAT POINT

As the name suggests, this area is full of islands and shoals. The clear water is treacherous, its depths uncharted. On the north shore there is a small jetty called Flat Point where Stephen (Etienne) Augustin Rochbert de la Morandiere operated an independent fur trading post before resettling to Killarney in the 1820s.

Years later, in the early 1900s, speculation abounded over why Harry Wright, a Detroit Professor of Ancient Languages, and his sister would choose to live here in seclusion. While idle gossip needed no fuel, the professor's sister likely fanned the flames with her reclusive nature and eccentric, old-fashioned clothing. Together they created an unusual farm devoted entirely to growing strawberries and flowers. Water piped from what is today Wright's Lake irrigated their garden, one of the first of its kind in the region. With the help of Finnish girls who worked in exchange for English lessons, the Wrights produced bumper crops for markets in Little Current and several tourist camps.

BARREN ISLAND

Contrary to its name, Barren Island was not dull at the turn of the twentieth century. Harry Hawkins from Blind River ran the fishing station by day and turned its net shed into a dance hall by night, attracting excursion boats from Little Current.

HOG ISLAND

Near the trading post run by the Hudson's Bay Company at La Cloche lies a group of small pastoral islands, including one originally dubbed Rattlesnake Island because of its abundant slithery population. It underwent a name change when an enterprising employee at the post had a bright idea: turn the island into a feeding ground for swine! There is nothing left at Hog Island except remains of the wooden wharves where goods were off-loaded from ships into canoes for the trip up river (see next site).

Fort La Cloche Trading Post

The entrance to the La Cloche River looks more like a creek when viewed from the North Channel, its gentle curves abloom with purple water iris and wild roses. Further upstream, the landscape opens to reveal several buildings clustered on the height of land. Here the fur trading post Fort La Cloche once stood. (The fort's history is complicated by the existence of two other posts bearing similar names: one built in 1790 on Great La Cloche Island, the other at the mouth of the La Cloche River.)

Fort La Cloche belonged to the North West Company, which was founded in 1783 by an independent group of Montreal fur merchants. In contrast to its rival, the royally-chartered Hudson's Bay Company, with posts clustered around Hudson Bay waiting for the Indians to come to them to trade, the NWC penetrated the interior, seeking out and expanding its network of Indian contacts. To facilitate the voyageurs' arduous journey from Montreal, it was vital to have an extensive system of trading posts such as La Cloche and Mississagi River. The intrepid men who travelled in *canots de maître*, thirty-five-foot freight canoes that could hold one hundred 90-pound fur packs and a crew of twelve, were more than traders. They were responsible for opening up and mapping vast new territories and placing them under the influence of the British Crown, out of reach of the newly-created American nation.

In exchange for axes, blankets, beads, guns, shot, and powder, pelts were collected throughout the season from Indians in the region or at an annual spring gathering at the

The old Hudson's Bay Post l to r: storehouse, store, servants' house, factor's house, clerks' house.

fort. The North West Company competed amicably with local free traders but maintained a fierce, frequently nasty rivalry with the Hudson's Bay Company. In 1816, this enmity finally erupted into violence at the Red River junction in Manitoba. Known as the Seven Oaks Massacre, the clash resulted in the deaths of Robert Semple, HBC chief and Governor of Rupert's Land and twenty of his settlers, but only one of the attacking band of Me´tis hunters who were allied with the NWC. The intense competition between the companies continued to escalate, placing a tremendous drain on the resources of both and so, in 1821, they amalgamated under the Hudson's Bay Company title. Although the NWC name disappeared, many of its chief factors and traders joined the HBC and helped move it into a new era of prosperity. Fort La Cloche became the HBC's district headquarters for Lake Huron with John McBean, a former Nor' Wester, as Chief Factor.

A brief sketch by travel writer Anna Jameson offers a glimpse of Fort La Cloche in 1837:

> Here we found the first and only signs of civilised society on our voyage . . . The factory consists of a large log-house, and extensive store to contain the goods bartered with the Indians, and huts inhabited by work people, hunters, voyageurs, and others; a small village, in short . . . The table was laid in their hall for supper, and we carried off, with their good-will, a large mess of broiled fish, dish and all, and can of milk, which delicious viands we discussed in our boat with great satisfaction.

Accounts of the annual trading ceremony at Fort La Cloche are missing but one can imagine it being a smaller version of the one at York Factory on Hudson Bay, described in *The Fur Trade and Western Canadian Society* by Frits Pannekoek:

> Several flotillas of canoes assembled out of sight of the Factory, each captained by a leader. The various leaders then exchanged gifts with the Chief Factor, and in ceremonies that lasted two or three days, they made speeches and smoked the pipe. Only after these ceremonies were completed did the actual trade begin. The exchange of goods was conducted through a window in the "trade room" and only one Indian was permitted in the room at a time, although their leader was allowed behind the trade window to ensure fair measure.

HBC Chief Factor McBean was understandably alarmed by new developments on Manitoulin Island that threatened his trade. Following the Treaty of 1836, the Indian

Department invited Indians from all over Upper Canada to settle on Manitoulin and be taught a trade or how to farm. These ideas were a threat to the HBC which wanted the natives to continue to trap and hunt and remain dependent on the company for supplies. If the Indians should also gain proficiency in English, they might be inclined to take control of their own affairs and trade directly with schooners at places like Collingwood and Penetanguishene, where they would have access to goods at fair market value rather than the inflated prices HBC traders offered.

In the following years profits began to slide. Non-native residents illegally set themselves up as independent traders and cashed in on their proximity to a population exceeding one thousand Indians by selling goods on credit throughout the year. Items, often advanced at five times original cost, locked the Indians into an endless cycle of debt.

No longer able to rely on natives coming to La Cloche to trade, the Hudson's Bay Company requested permission from the Indian Department to transfer their post to Manitoulin Island. In 1856 they established a store and a wharf at Little Current. Shortly thereafter they were accused by a special government commission of destroying the livelihood of Ojibwe businessman George Abbotossway. The Indian Department ordered the HBC to leave and in 1857 they returned to La Cloche. (For more about the strife between the HBC and George Abbotossway see Little Current p.54).

As the HBC's most southerly post, La Cloche remained active until the HBC district headquarters was transferred to Sudbury in 1885, with the coming of the Canadian Pacific Railway. The La Cloche premises were leased to the lumber firm J. & T. Conlon of Thorold (whose mill ruins still stand near Little Current on Picnic Island). After Conlon left in 1892, the old fort became a favourite picnic site for residents of nearby Massey. Over the years, the buildings suffered repeated vandalism. Floors and walls were torn out for firewood, and eventually Fort La Cloche was marked only by an overgrown graveyard, a few stone foundations, and a half-toppled chimney. The T. Eaton Company bought the site to build a lodge for their executives, later selling out to a private sportsman's club. It was next converted into a Junior Rangers camp by the Ministry of Natural Resources. Today the Spanish River First Nation owns the site.

WRECK OF THE *IROQUOIS*

Sailing through the McBean Channel is very tranquil: few boats, fewer cottages and beautiful surroundings. In 1902 when the wooden steamer *Iroquois* was built, the air was filled with the sounds of sawmills rather than the lonely call of loons. Owned by the Goderich Engine and Bicycle Company, the 112-ft. (33.6m) *Iroquois* steamed along with twelve passengers and a cargo of supplies destined for Manitoulin Island. As they approached East Rock, a fire engulfed the ship and within an hour the burning hulk slid to the silty bottom. Passengers and crew escaped in lifeboats to Spanish Mills (Little Detroit). Only the burned-out hull remains, in 25 ft. (7.5m) of water. To find it, search south of the green marker known as East Rock. It is possible to see it from the surface, but it is better to dive around the area.

CROKER ISLAND

A Magnetic Island and Old Quarry

In 1963 a federal-provincial aero-magnetic survey disclosed the presence of a large circular magnetic anomaly over Croker, Benjamin and Fox Islands. Unlike the neighbouring Benjamin Islands, Croker is not formed of granite but is predominately a younger rock called syenitic which is made up of about twelve different minerals and is often deep red in colour.

North Channel circular magnetic anomalies

Scientists believe the Croker Island rock intruded about 1,450 million years ago, meaning that before parts of the island crystallized, hot magma spewed up and "intruded" into it. The rock is reportedly similar to some found at Mount Dromedary in Australia and at Gibson Peak in California. As copper and nickel are often associated with this type of rock, Croker's mineral content was investigated, but concentrations were too low to be commercially viable.

On the southern tip of the island, near a long, diagonal striation in the rock, one can see traces of a rock quarry dating back to the 1920s, when blocks were cut for construction of the Book-Cadillac Hotel in Detroit. Old machinery, a boiler and rotted dock pilings beneath the water are all that are left.

BENJAMIN ISLANDS

Heralded as the most beautiful grouping of islands on the North Channel, the Benjamins' red granite rises from the water's edge in smooth, majestic, undulating curves. Pines grow out of bare rock. From a high point on South Benjamin, the delightful shapes of the Sow and Pigs Islands point south-west to Clapperton Island. The former lightkeeper of the Clapperton lighthouse was Benjamin Baker, after whom these tranquil islands were named.

From 1875 to 1894, the educated and enterprising Baker operated not only the lighthouse but also a successful farm. When he could not find the right kind of jars in which to can meat, he paid the Dominion Glass Co. to

Benjamin Baker disappeared, 1894

manufacture a series to his own design. Family records show that Baker had at least three wives, although death records have been found for only two of them. The greatest mystery however revolves around his own death. Following an evening on the town with the boys in Gore Bay, he had failed to return to the lighthouse. His sailboat was sighted drifting down the channel by his son, but other than his dog, an empty wallet and a whiskey bottle, there was no sign of Baker. His body was never found and no explanation was ever offered by anyone in Gore Bay. The whiskey bottle sat on a shelf for years until Baker's daughter-in-law took a medicinal swig and immediately became violently ill. Were the contents poisoned? No one will ever know.

HOOK ISLAND'S FOSSILS

Offshore, Hook Island does not seem particularly remarkable. But appearances are deceiving. Closely viewed, the limestone reveals subtle hues of gray, pale blue and yellow. Huge stone slabs hang out over the lake and underneath, waves gurgle and crash against the shore. Modern explorers will be rewarded by an astounding array of fossils known as Nautiloids, some up to a foot in length. They look like segmented worms with tapered ends but what you are in fact examining are the fossilized remains of a shell, from which a squid-like head protruded at one end. Its tentacle-like arms (it did not have suckers like an octopus) were used to pull food towards its partially-hidden, beaked mouth.

In 1970, an old fisherman reported to the Lake Huron Fisheries Assessment Unit:

> . . . Alan [Morphet] said that it was the greatest place for fossils he had ever seen. He said that there was a fossil there—he knew about it—it was like a man; only it had fins and a tail. I think he said it was in six or eight feet of water. Anyway, someone around there got wise to it and they tried to get the thing and broke it all to pieces. Alan told me about it and I believe him. He isn't the kind of guy to stretch it.

Hook Island's limestone is formed largely of calcium and dolomite sediments. The fossilized creatures are from a time when a shallow tropical sea covered most of southern Ontario, some 450 million years ago. (For more fossils see West Neebish p.238).

EMMA E. THOMPSON/THOMAS J. CAHOON WRECKS

On the north side of Innis Island, close to Hesson Point, lies the wreck of the *Emma E. Thompson*. On May 28, 1914, this 260-ton wooden steamer was taking a load of lumber from the French River mills on Georgian Bay to Saginaw, Michigan, when an intense storm blew up. Seeking shelter, she hid behind Innis Island. A fire broke out and the eleven-man crew had to escape to the island.

Today the 125-ft. (38m) ship is sitting upright on the silty bottom in less than 30 ft. (9m) of water. This is a great wreck for all divers, and under certain conditions, it can be seen by snorkelers. Even though the wreck burned, there is still much to explore: rudder, chains, pumps, tools and the nearly intact bow section with three sets of anchor chains. To find the wreck, look just south of Hesson Point. As you look back towards the point, line it up with the farther Royal Point, then put your head over the side with a mask. It is sometimes marked with a plastic jug.

If weather is good and you are interested in finding another wreck, try looking for the schooner *Thomas J. Cahoon*, located between Kenny Shoal and Kenny Point on Innis Island. It is quite broken up but still retains a center-board and a visible bow and stern. It lies in less than twenty feet of water.

DARCH ISLAND

Heroics of Early Mail Delivery

To understand the history of Darch Island, look beyond the sandy cove, the beautiful beach and the quaint old wooden cabin perched beside the harbour (open year round to boaters and skidooers). Instead, visualize a frozen expanse stretching to the horizon under a piercing blue sky with swirls of snow dancing over patches of open ice. For the Island's story takes place in winter, during the years when mail was delivered across the frozen North Channel, first by dogsled and then by horse-drawn sleigh.

Postal delivery was never taken for granted in this region, as each letter represented a life risked. In the 1850s, mail was distributed from Penetanguishene in southern Georgian Bay by Indians hauling about 180 pounds of mail on their sleds. Letters were either three weeks late, or never received. (No one knows what happened to the lonely courier and his dog team from Penetanguishene who was last spotted drifting on an ice floe.)

The Gore Bay mail sleigh

It was an occupation for the hardy. The mail courier for Bruce Mines, Mr. Miron, snowshoed to Killarney to meet the Penetanguishine courier. He claimed he wore out one pair of snowshoes on the way there and another on the way back. Depending on the weather, he could cover between 35 and 60 miles a day (He later confessed that he would often try to leave before the Penetang courier's arrival so that he could return home without the burden of mail on his back!) After meeting up with Miron, the Penetanguishine courier would then complete his bone-chilling trek by crossing over to Manitoulin. On the island, mail was distributed by whatever means possible. Boys could earn extra pocket money by couriering mail, but it was not easy. Delivery from Little Current to Manitowaning could take anywhere from one to two-and-a-half days by snowshoe.

Around 1900, trains would deliver the winter mail to Spanish and Massey where it was loaded on horse-drawn sleighs for the hazardous trip across the channel to Gore Bay and Little Current. Many a harrowing night was spent travelling in circles when blizzards obliterated all trace of the snow-road. If it proved futile to proceed, the horses would be tied to the leeward side of the sleigh while the teamster huddled under a buffalo robe and prayed for dawn.

Late spring and early winter were the most feared times of the year. One mail courier, James Purvis, lost nine teams in thirty-one years. Horses wore special nooses around their necks so that if they fell through the ice, the driver had some chance of pulling them out. Too often, however, the horses would keep pawing through the weak ice, eventually drowning from exhaustion and exposure. In spring, the sleigh was usually replaced by a smaller sled-punt combination. This allowed horse, driver and mail to be ferried across stretches of open water.

From 1896 to 1930, Purvis was kept busy juggling his various business enterprises: a winter mail contract, a passenger sleigh service between Gore Bay and Spanish and a freight handling service. The sleigh would leave Gore Bay for Spanish at 7:00 a.m. and complete the round trip by 7:00 p.m. In order to maintain this rigorous schedule, Purvis used Darch Island as a halfway stop. Teamsters would hitch up a fresh team of horses while passengers stretched their legs and sipped a steaming cup of tea offered by the couple who tended the animals corralled on Darch.

PORTER CHAMBERLAIN/H. J. WEBB WRECKS

Fire was an ever-present threat on the North Channel. For the crew of the wooden steamer *Porter Chamberlain*, November 11, 1901 had been a hard day. Having loaded

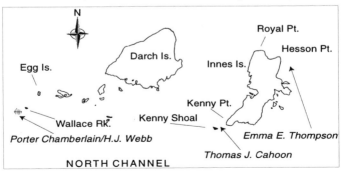

lumber and towed the schooner *H. J. Webb* (also loaded with lumber) through the blowing snow, they were approaching Darch Island when a fire started in the galley and quickly spread, engulfing both vessels. As the crew escaped to Belleau Island, the burning hulls drifted onto a shoal known as Wallace Rock.

Today the wreck is a large site that includes propeller blades, a centerboard and a boiler. To find the site, look west of Darch Island just south of Egg Island to the spot marked on maps as Wallace Rock. It is just west of the breaking water. When we found the site, we were lucky to have a calm day with the sun at our backs. As our bow cut through the water the boiler appeared like a whale surfacing before us.

BOYD ISLAND

Floeing Through the Night

Like so many of the lighthouses on Georgian Bay and the North Channel, Boyd Island had more than its share of near-disasters involving lightkeepers. William Martin (1829-1905) had the harrowing experience of finding himself icebound while rowing back from the mainland. His boat, locked between two ice floes, had been at the complete mercy of the powerful current which swept him right past his despairing wife on Boyd Island. Good fortune smiled, however, when he landed safely on Clapperton Island and, thanks to his wife's distress signal, he was found by a rescue team the next day, frost-bitten but otherwise unharmed.

Erected in 1885, the Boyd Island lighthouse met an ugly end in the 1960s. A Coast Guard crew poured forty-five gallons of gas into glass jars and set them on the window ledges. A fire was lit at the bottom of the house and the glass jars at the top were ignited by a bullet shot from a boat offshore.

AIRD ISLAND: SPANISH MILLS

During its peak in the 1920s, Spanish Mills had a population of over two hundred. Located on the east end of Aird Island, the village shared the same rough-hewn character as company towns on John Island and Spragge. Ron Brown's *Ghost Towns of Ontario* describes Spanish Mills as being composed of a dozen simple wooden houses for management and several boarding houses for single men, along with a school, church, dance hall and McNeil's store. Twenty different logging companies kept the Spanish Mills Lumber Company busy. When the company moved out in 1927, the village collapsed and became a virtual ghost town overnight. The majority of residents waited until

Village of Spanish Mills on Aird Island

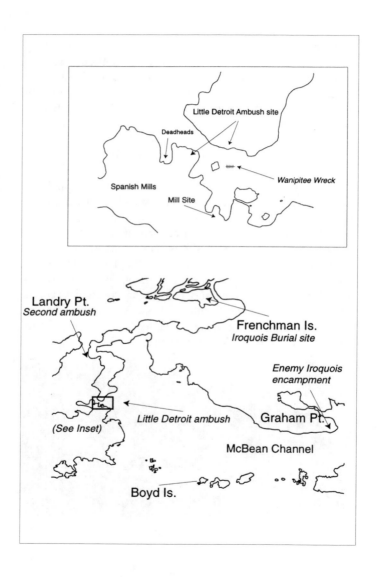

Little Detroit Ambush site

Deadheads

Wanipitee Wreck

Spanish Mills

Mill Site

Landry Pt.
Second ambush

Frenchman Is.
Iroquois Burial site

Enemy Iroquois
encampment

Little Detroit ambush

Graham Pt.

(See Inset)

McBean Channel

Boyd Is.

winter, then skidded their homes across the ice to Spanish.
The few buildings that remained either rotted or burned.
Next to the rock in the middle of the Little Detroit channel lie the remains of a small tug called the *Wanipitee* in
less than 20 ft. (6m) of water. To find it, look for the rock
with an iron ring on it. (Good luck with the dark sawdust-
filled water.)

LITTLE DETROIT

The Ojibwe Outwit Iroquois Warriors

Along the Spanish River in the mid 1600s, the Ojibwe
elder had a disturbing vision—fierce, merciless Iroquois
were coming, bringing with them a river of blood. A
reconnaissance team was quickly dispatched and returned
with the distressing news that the vision was only too true.
Iroquois had been spotted massing on Graham Point (the
southern point of the present day Spanish River First
Nation).

A plan of offence was drawn up. The chief knew the
one place from which the Ojibwe could launch an effective attack was a narrow passageway between the mainland and Aird Island, now called Little Detroit. But how
could they entice the Iroquois to pass through?

The plan involved using the Ojibwe women as decoys.
They were told to paddle their canoes out into the open
water a fair distance from Little Detroit, while the men
concealed themselves among the trees and crevasses flank-
ing each side of the sheer rock passage. This would be an
excellent vantage point from which to launch a surprise
assault.

Iroquois warriors attacked Ojibwe on the North Channel after the Huron were pushed out of Georgian Bay in 1649.

Meanwhile, in the Iroquois camp, an elder gifted with prophecy warned that he had heard terrible thunder, and predicted that no one who left the encampment at Graham Point would return alive. The arrogant Iroquois warriors blinded by their many successes, dismissed the premonition as foolishness.

Soon after, an Iroquois scout reported seeing a number of Ojibwe canoes. The Iroquois prepared to launch an attack. As their canoes slipped into Little Detroit, a war cry cracked the stillness. From all sides, rocks poured down like lightning bolts on the unsuspecting Iroquois who desperately tried to escape by swimming to shore. But the high walls of Little Detroit prevented them from landing. They met their deaths swiftly.

Those warriors who did escape the carnage were caught in a second ambush further up the channel at Landry Point. Some of the slain were taken to Frenchman Island at the mouth of the Spanish River where, it is said, tormented Iroquois souls could be heard wandering the island and crying. The rest were quickly buried on the spot, as the Ojibwe feared that other Iroquois, on seeing their fallen brethren, would try to avenge their deaths. Their fears were well-founded. (For the second part of this battle, see Spanish River First Nation below.)

SPANISH RIVER FIRST NATION

As a provision of the Robinson-Huron Treaty, the 28,000-acre Spanish River Reserve was created at the mouth of the River on September 9, 1850. It was an area already rich in Indian lore. Ninety years earlier, on a tip of land called Sagamok Point, a group of Iroquois marauders gathered to lick their wounds after being ambushed by Ojibwe on Aird Island. While they waited for reinforcements, they planned their revenge.

The Ojibwe who had set up camp inland were shaken by

Spanish River family, mill (l) and St. Joseph's School(r).

the news that a large group of Iroquois had been spied at Sagamok Point. Chief Maw-tig-mish ordered defence preparations immediately. He instructed his men to dig shoulder-deep fox holes, and the women and children to prepare sleeping accommodations in the storage huts.

Armed with Ojibwe weapons and a few muskets, the warriors kept silent watch from their deep hiding places. As the Iroquois crept closer to what they thought was a sleeping village, the night air was split; the Ojibwe warrior, Me-ow-us, fired first, killing the Iroquois Chief's two sons. The Iroquois retreated, regrouped, then attacked a second time. Once again they were repelled by the determined Ojibwe men, women, and children, who pelted the Iroquois with rocks as they fled into the woods.

SPANISH: WHAT'S IN A NAME?

According to legend, around the year 1750, Ojibwe warriors penetrated south-west to Spanish-occupied territories. On their return to the North Channel, they brought with them a ravishing *senorita* who married a local chief and bore him a large family. Today there are still descendants bearing the name Espaniole, and the towns of Spanish and Espanola.

Spanish's hopes of becoming a booming lumber village waned as Blind River and Espanola successfully attracted the larger milling companies. In 1902, a railway station was built and the village's focus shifted to becoming a small service centre for the Canadian Pacific Railway. A long-awaited economic boost came in February 1911 when a fire destroyed Wikwemikong's missionary school on Manitoulin Island. The Church was eager to build another school but wanted the new one separate from the Wikwemikong community and on the rail line. Spanish residents were delighted when the Jesuits purchased an acre at the mouth of the Spanish River and erected St. Peter Claver's School (later Garnier College) for 180 boys, and St. Joseph's School for 150 girls.

Although the origins of the town's name may have been romantic, for some First Nations children, the name was anything but. In 1936, Basil Johnston and his four-year-old sister were brought to the school from their Cape Croker home by an Indian Agent as part of his quota. In his book *Indian School Days* Basil Johnston remembers:

> The word or the name 'Spanish' might seem to be not more filled with menace than any other word; but it inspired dread from the very first that we Indian boys heard it . . . Spanish was a place of woe for miscreants, just like hell and purgatory were for sinners.

Boys at the Residential School

The goal of the residential school was to prepare boys for vocations such as tailoring, blacksmithing, shoemaking, tin-smithing even though by Johnston's graduation these trades were no longer in demand. Garnier closed in 1958, and St. Joseph's in 1962.

The town enjoyed a boom during the 50s and 60s. In 1956, Noranda Inc. opened a Sulphuric Acid Plant on the Indian Reserve at Cutler. As only chief officials were allowed to live on the reserve, Noranda purchased land at the east end of Spanish to build a town site for its employees. This boosted the population to 12,000 and gave Spanish the injection of life it needed. As Spanish was the nearest community to the mines up the Elliot Lake Road, it also became the transportation centre for mail and freight.

JOHN ISLAND: HOME TO THE STOLEN MILL

From stolen mill to spectacular fire to YMCA summer camp. In a nut shell, that is the history of John Island, one of the North Channel's most remarkable settlements. The large mixed forest island was bought by the nefarious Moiles brothers—Jim, George, Henry and Charles—to escape creditors threatening to seize their mill in DeTour, Michigan.

This was the stuff of legends: stealing off with an American sawmill and moving it to Canada under cover of darkness. But it was hardly a solid foundation for trust. Many local loggers, and more that a few of the mill's U. S. customers were wary of dealing with the Moiles brothers. Times were tough and competition was fierce as several local mills all vied for the same markets. Two years after the hijacked lumber mill arrived from Michigan, workers were still earning little more than room and board. By

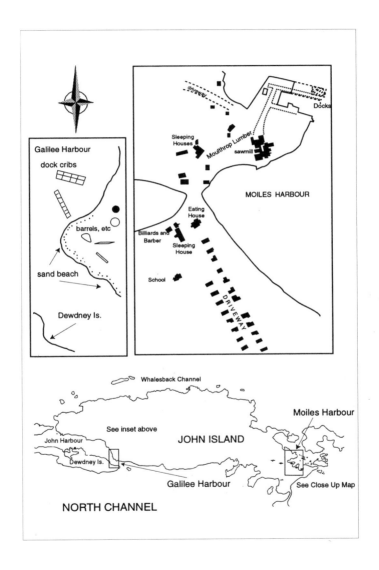

1903 the brothers admitted defeat and sold the operation to Guy Moulthrop of Bay City, Michigan.

The new owner left his footprints on the area (considerable as they were at size 16) but little else. Occupied with business interests elsewhere, Moulthrop was rarely on the Island. Nevertheless he saw that the mill flourished under skilled management. At its peak the mill employed only sixty men, making it one of the smallest of the twelve sawmills operating in the area. Workers and their families lived in company-owned houses on a main street that followed the curve of Moiles Harbour. Drinking water from a nearby spring flowed through a pipe underneath the boardwalk running down its centre. But the heart of the town was the baseball field, where mill workers played teams from Cutler, Spragge, Spanish Mills, and Blind River.

The hamlet's most prominent feature was sand, a decidedly mixed blessing. For swimmers it was wonderful. For homeowners it was a nightmare. Five inches of sand lay on the main street just waiting for a strong wind to scatter it

Old dock pilings still visible in Moiles Harbour

Worker's home on sand-covered road

between buildings and in living rooms as well.

To combat their isolation, the townspeople thought up many ways to keep busy. One of the most popular activities took place in a secluded poker shack (until authorities came over from Webbwood on the North Shore and ruined the fun). Saturday was dance night. Accordion and fiddle players set the tempo and no one missed a dance. And so it was that on April 17, 1918, while oblivious villagers kicked up their heels, the mill caught fire.

By dawn it was a smoking ruin. Some residents shrugged in resignation; others wept in despair. Soon after, the majority packed up and abandoned John Island. In an ironic echo of the mill's origins almost three decades earlier, workers dismantled most of the surviving buildings and shipped them off to the mainland.

By the 1950s, the 278 acres of John Island were owned by a Senator Bell. After his death, the local YMCA sought to buy the land for use as a summer camp. A price of

$3,000 was quoted by his widow and after a good deal of effort, the YMCA succeeded in raising the necessary funds. At this point, Mrs. Bell deeded the land to the organization for one dollar and told it to keep the money it had raised.

Exploring John Island is fascinating, but watch for "mutant" poison ivy. Unlike the more familiar variety, the plants are unusually large and just as undesirable. At the mill site, only the massive crumbling stone wall of the sawdust burner still stands enclosing a pit thirty-feet deep. The original ballpark, reputedly one of the oldest in the province, is still used by the YMCA campers. Large dock pilings extend out into Moiles Harbour which remains littered with dock planking from the mill's extensive pier and railway. One of the rail cars can be seen at the camp, together with artifacts collected from the mill and town. (For the adventures of how the stolen mill reached John Island see DeTour, p.210).

WHALESBACK CHANNEL

Henry Wolsey Bayfield joined the British Navy in 1806 at the age of eleven. By 1815 he was a lieutenant well on his way to becoming a meticulous surveyor. In 1816, at the age of twenty-one he was sent from England to chart the islands and shorelines of the Canadian Great Lakes.

The survey was carried out by a crew crammed into two, six-oared rowboats, loaded with enough provisions to last six weeks. Comfortable it was not:

> I slept in all weathers in the Boat, or on the shore upon
> a Buffaloe robe under the Boat's mainsail thrown over
> a few branches placed on the ground. Many a night
> have I slept in this way, when the Thermometer was

down near Zero, and sometimes even below it. Yet
even this was not so wearing as trying to sleep, in vain,
in the warm nights of summer . . . in the smoke of a fire
to keep off the clouds of Moschettoes which literally
darkened the air.

When he ran out of names of royalty and naval officers
to give to the hundreds of islands he surveyed, Bayfield
resorted to those of lower-ranked soldiers and sailors, rel-
atives, friends, ships, local residents, and even shapes.
Whalesback Channel for example was so named because
the beautifully streamlined rock that flanks this passage
reminded him of sailing the Atlantic Ocean.

Although Bayfield's contribution was extremely important, his shoreline charts did not indicate water depths or
shoals. This partly contributed to the deaths of four hundred and seventy lives lost on the Great Lakes between
1879 and 1882, prompting the government to initiate a
more detailed survey. In 1883, in the *Bayfield,* a 120-ft.
(36-m) wooden tug, Captain John Boulton began this ten-
year project.

In each two-man row boat, one sailor worked the oars
while the other hung a depth-measuring lead line from the
bow and made notes. Like Bayfield's crew, Boulton's men
often suffered from the extreme weather conditions. At
one point they threatened to halt the survey because of the
vicious black flies. In the summer of 1887, fifty years after
Bayfield's survey, Boulton reached Whalesback Channel.
He was pleasantly surprised to find the namesake rock
free of hated insects, thanks to an offshore breeze. After
pulling the steamer alongside, the crew camped on the tail
of Bayfield's whale for a month, swimming and fishing at
the completion of each long day's survey.

JOHN ISLAND

Galilee Fishing Station

At Galilee, the fishing station was owned by James P. McDonald who had fished from the age of thirteen until his retirement at seventy-three. Waters around John Island had long been famous for their rich stocks of trout, pickerel and walleye but no one had ever lifted $14,000 worth of whitefish in three days, before McDonald accomplished that feat in 1919. Overnight he became one of the richest men in Blind River where he built a house in the affluent neighbourhood then nicknamed "Silk Stocking Hill" (now Lakeside Avenue). Old-timer Charlie Quinn recalled J. P.:

> I liked him very much—they called him a scrooge but he was none of that. He made money and he looked after his money. He paid his bills and never asked anyone to work for nothing. One time my grandfather took over six or seven bags of vegetables to McDonald, and J. P. was short twenty-five cents. My grandfather said 'that's okay.' 'No,' he said, 'it isn't okay; if you owe me a quarter I want it, if I owe you a quarter I want to pay it.' That was the kind of man he was.

At the height of his fishing enterprise, McDonald owned five steam tugs and employed fifteen men at his fishing station. Today, dock cribs and black smudges on the rocks are reminders of the tar once used by those fishermen to protect their nets. Metal hoops from barrels which once were used to transport salted fish to market rust in heaps in the woods. For the boater, Galilee makes an idyllic anchorage after a day of cruising.

SERPENT HARBOUR AND RIVER

Sea Serpent

Ojibwe believe that the subterranean tunnels criss-cross-ing Manitoulin Island are the paths by which a water monster called Mishebeshu (*mishe*, "great or big," and *beshu*, "lynx") gains access to the inland lakes. This creature is pictured in two ways: one has a large cat's head with horns and a long scaly tail, the other is a huge sea serpent. In *The Island of the Anishnaabeg*, author Theresa Smith comments on this seeming inconsistency,

> None of my (Manitoulin Island) consultants knew of any reason why they thought of Mishebeshu as both huge water cat and a serpent. Mishebeshu is just, in the original sense of the word, a true monster (from Latin *monstrum*, "something marvelous") sharing the worldwide mythic patterns of dragons and super-natural serpents.

Depending on the time of year, some elders feign ignorance about Mishebeshu. They prefer to reserve any discussion for winter when the monster is trapped beneath the ice, rather than possibly provoking him by speaking his name in summer. They fear Mishebeshu's cruelty, his ability to stir up treacherous waters with his powerful tail and an evil habit of drowning his victims.

One of Mishebeshu's underwater dens is said to be near the mouth of the Serpent River. A former resident of the old waterfront village of Spragge, Mrs. Day, certainly believed this to be true. As recounted to Tom Haddow of *The Standard* in 1983, she was familiar with a native legend about a thirteen-year-old boy who vanished after being left on Herman's Point during a vision quest. Evidently, weeks after the mysterious disappearance, hunters noticed a great commotion in Serpent's Harbour. A large serpent with the boy clinging to its back rose out of the water. For the Ojibwe, the sighting confirmed that the boy had been forced into the spirit world.

Although many years had passed, Mrs. Day was convinced something strange was still going on. How else to explain why several swimmers had disappeared in the harbour? Mrs. Day spoke of hearing weird sounds and finding odd objects on her rooftop. Concerned for the safety of her children, she convinced her husband to move from Spragge in 1934. When asked by Haddow what might be behind the strange circumstances, she replied: "It's that serpent . . . that place is really haunted." Another 65- year-old interviewee, described an even closer encounter: ". . . suddenly about a half mile from shore the boat started to

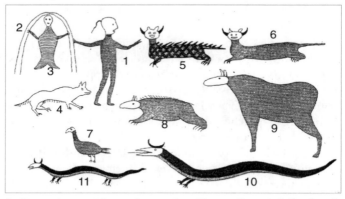

Indian pictographs redrawn by Henry Rowe Schoolcraft: 5)Mishebeshu (crosses on body denote power by night) 6) power in daylight 10) great serpent 11) great serpent with legs. Both lynx and serpent are Mishebeshu

rock. We held on to the side . . . the water began to boil as if something was trying to get to the surface."

We first encountered the possibility of a water monster while reading interviews conducted in 1970 by the Lake Huron Fisheries Assessment Unit. Fishermen were asked whether they had ever sighted such a creature. While they all replied in the negative, we thought it curious the government had even posed the question. Retired fishermen, John Hillis, told us that while he did not necessarily believe in the monster himself, he knew many who did. Our research uncovered three compelling "Mishebeshu" accounts. This affidavit was signed by eight Lake Ontario voyageurs who at first thought they were paddling towards a burnt log:

> . . . We continued toward it until within thirty yards, the animal raised its head about ten feet out of the water, looking around him in the most awful and ferocious manner, and darting forward with great velocity, making the water fly in every direction, and throwing columns at a vertical height of seven or eight feet with its tail. After having gone in a western direction about one or two miles, he appeared to resume his former state, we then resolved to attack him, and accordingly loaded our guns for this purpose, and moved slowly toward him with a shotgun. We here had a good view of the animal, he is at least thirty-seven feet long, two-and-a-half feet in diameter, is covered with black scales which a musket ball has but little effect on . . . he had a tremendous head and similar to that of a com-

mon snake—frequently thrusting from his mouth
a large red and venomous looking tongue.

In 1821, the *Boston Gazette* offered a hefty $10,000
reward for any individual who caught this sea serpent.

A second sighting reported in the 1896 *Marine Record*
spoke of two settlers, John Brasser and his brother, who
were crossing from Sugar Island on the St. Mary's River to
the mainland. They spotted something that looked like a
drowned man. On closer inspection it turned out to be a
snake about fifteen feet long. The "horned-lynx" had, ". .
. eyes . . . at the extreme sides of the head and over them
two bony protuberances stuck out about three inches."
Seeing the men, it whirled and went after the boat. They
rowed for their lives. After fetching a rifle, they returned to
the same location. Again the creature seemed ready to
attack. They fired. It raised its head several feet out of the
water then fell over on its side and disappeared.

The most recent of the three sightings occurred in 1946.
Bess Munroe, social hostess aboard the *City of Detroit III*
reported a sixty-foot sea serpent covered in scales with a
huge horned head. This description was confirmed by
more than a dozen passengers and several crew. The
Central Press Dispatch of Detroit wrote:

> The travellers sighted the thing as the ship was enter-
> ing the bay near Flowerpot Island, en route to
> Midland. It came within 500 feet of the ship and
> remained in sight for approximately fifteen minutes,
> they said. Then it disappeared into the rain and fog.

Whether myth or fact, the belief in the existence of a Great
Lakes sea monster persists.

SPRAGGE

Fatality of the Great Depression

Along the quiet north shore of Serpent Harbour stand a few traces of the former sawmill village of Spragge: stone foundations of the mill and powerhouse and a graveyard. It was first named Cook's Mill after the founding brothers Hiram and George Cook who built a sawmill here in 1882. It was renamed Spragge (after the township) by the Waldie Brothers, Fred, Robert and William, who bought the mill in 1906 and operated successful logging camps along the Mississagi, Serpent and Blind Rivers. It was a grave disappointment to the community when they opted to tow the logs to their Victoria Harbour mill in southern Georgian Bay.

Luckily, McFadden and Malloy Company reopened the mill in 1913. Astute businessmen, the new owners hit upon an idea for a tax shelter by running pipes from two boilers in the company's machine house to provide steam heating for the whole town. As Spragge was primarily built on rock, the exposed pipes were covered by three-foot-high boxes and filled with planer shavings from the mill to protect them from freezing in winter. Former resident, Lyle Marcellus, remembers the fun of running across the tops of those steam boxes, despite the severe reprimand that always followed.

Another favourite memory was of the 1926 Pierce-Arrow touring car owned by James J. McFadden: "It had a sand body, black fenders, running boards, step pads, black wooden wheels, yellow pin striped spokes, whitewall tires, a sand-coloured top, black cushion seats in leather, of course, and an amber-coloured windshield and side glass. The three-beam headlights were built into the fenders." When it rolled into

Panorama of Spragge

town, boys crowded around in hopes of being taken for a ride. McFadden often treated them, along with his two pet German Shepherds, to ice cream cones from the parlour located in the pool hall (which also served as an overflow school).

By 1926 Spragge's population had grown to three hundred. Dominating the town was a twenty-room summer residence built high on the hill by McFadden. There was also a house for the chauffeur and a seven-car garage for his many cars. As a counterpoint, Spragge could boast the requisite number of hermit dwellings. "Old Jerry" Dacey lived in a little hut attached to his chicken coop. The entrance door was made of heavy planks and was latched, barred and bolted from the inside. On the edge of town were two other hermits, Markus Herman and Charlie Hill, whose abode was constructed from railway ties and graced by a sod-covered tin roof that grew a lush pate of grass each summer.

When McFadden and Malloy closed the mill in 1932, dozens of men were thrown into the growing ranks of the

Waldie Brothers Lumber Co., 1908

unemployed. The mood became sombre. As the town was fearing for its future without its major employer, a fire started in the lumberyard. Lyle Marcellus was there that September day and recalled,

> The fire started at 9:00 a.m. in the west end yard with a hell of west wind blowing. Along with it went 75% of the town. . . It was terrifying. At that time . . . there was no fire fighting equipment, and by the time the Lands and Forests got their fighters from Blind River . . . much of the town was gone.

Panicked townspeople tossed their furniture onto lumber wagons, and drove to the baseball field where they loaded everything onto empty CPR cars and pulled away from the reach of the fire. By 9:00 p.m. most of Spragge had been reduced to a smouldering mess. Ironically, the mill survived.

McFadden and Malloy helped some of the dispossessed by towing company houses and a store from their closed North Shore mill at Nestorville (another Depression casualty). By

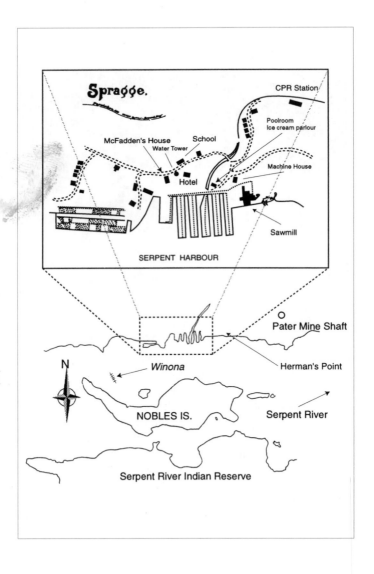

fall, the school had been rebuilt. Life, however uncertain, went on although most of Spragge's residents were on relief. The following year, the mill caught fire. No one raised an eyebrow. Many had secretly assumed the first fire had been a badly botched attempt by the company to boost their bottom line with insurance money. As Mr. Marcellus remembered with a wry chuckle, "All mills in the Depression burned down—conveniently."

In order to collect the insurance claim McFadden and Malloy had to rebuild the mill. There was, however, no stipulation that the job had to be a good one. The mill never reopened and Spragge began its slow decline. People moved away in search of work. Houses were moved elsewhere or torn down. Eventually the mill was dismantled, and scrap collectors cleared out the rest, including all the piping that criss-crossed through town. In the 50s, the uranium mining boom around Elliot Lake brought a short-lived resurgence to Spragge, as did the discovery of copper in 1953. Today only a smattering of houses remain. On a recent visit, Marcellus walked along the Serpent Harbour shoreline and observed that the ". . . ground was clean as a pin—you would never even know a town stood there."

Wreck of the S. S. *Winona*

As the *Winona* pitched and rolled, the mail bags on her deck thumped from side to side. No way, thought the Captain. Manitoulin would have to wait until tomorrow for its mail. With spray pounding the wheelhouse in buckets, he commanded the wheelsman to turn the 158-foot *Winona* around and head back to Spragge. When they returned to the dock the mail was taken ashore for the night. Luckily. At 2:00 a.m. the captain awoke with a start. Did he smell smoke? Alerted, the passengers and crew ran from their quarters and were met by a ball of fire. Somehow they started the water pumps but overwhelmed by smoke and flames, many jumped ship. The blaze roared through the *Winona*'s windows and began eating at the dock. Envisioning a wharf, town, and forest in flames, the Captain bellowed to cut her loose.

Instead of heading south into the bay, the *Winona* was driven eastward by the wind toward the J. J. McFadden Company wharves where inviting piles of milled wood awaited shipment. Seeing the lumber stock threatened, the company dispatched their gas boat to tow the flaming hulk across the bay onto a shoal where she finished burning and sank. Her 29 years of service (1902-31) were over.

Winona caught fire at the Spragge Dock, 1931

A buoy now marks the spot where the Winona's *ribs can still be seen. It is easily accessible to snorkelers although the water is dark and visibility is less than 3 ft. Care should be taken to remain visible to boating traffic. In seasons of low water the top of the wreck is awash.*

ALGOMA MILLS

The Banff Springs Hotel That Never Came To Be

During the late 1800s, the North Shore was abuzz. The Canadian Pacific Railway had won the contract to construct a railway to connect Canada from east to west. On the North Shore, work centred around the link between Sudbury and Algoma Mills. Labourers poured in to clear trees, build road beds, lay ties and steel rails, while local sawmills worked overtime to satisfy the demands. At Algoma Mills, the CPR purchased two hundred acres for a proposed rail terminus, in anticipation of the steamers that would link Algoma Mills to the lakehead at Thunder Bay (then Fort William). Plans were drawn up for wharves, rail yards, grain elevators, freight sheds and a 300-room hotel.

As part of its advertising strategy, the CPR had begun to promote itself as "The World's Greatest Travel System." Tourists needed only book once if they wished rail, steamer or hotel accommodations. Algoma Mills was chosen as a depot from which rail passengers could embark on one of the new, elegant CPR passenger-cargo steamers being built in Scotland. In 1882, the completed *Athabasca, Algoma* and *Alberta* sailed to Montreal where they were cut in half in order to fit through the lock system. They were then towed

Algoma, one of the three C.P.R. passenger steamers

to Buffalo and reassembled before completing the journey to
the North Shore in 1884. Freight could now be sent from
Montreal to Algoma Mills by rail, continue on to Fort
William by steamer and arrive in Winnipeg by rail after a
sixty-six hour journey of 1,320 miles.

Plans for the CPR's Algoma Mills Hotel had been drafted,
locals were hired to collect boulders, and construction of its
massive foundations begun when rumours started to circulate
that the future of the rail line was in doubt. Speculation gave
way to fact. The CPR had altered its route so that the main
rail line diverged long before reaching Algoma Mills. The
town was left with only a branch line. All work on the railway west of Algoma Mills was abandoned, as was work on
the grain elevator because it would have been in direct competition with another one under construction in Owen Sound.

Nevertheless, the CPR still strongly believed in the tourism
potential of Algoma Mills. Although strong, its support for
the hotel project was soon crushed under the weight of political pressure from the west. The hotel site was to be shifted
from the North Channel to Banff in the Rocky Mountains.

Today the Banff Springs Hotel is perhaps the best known hotel in the country. One wonders what the future of Algoma Mills and the North Channel might have been if the hotel had been constructed. Instead, Algoma Mills became a CPR district coaling depot, its scenic panorama filled with cranes, mounds of coal and barges piled high with the messy fuel.

Another blow came when the eastern terminus for the CPR's Great Lakes Steamship Service was transferred to Owen Sound. Algoma Mills was relegated to the status of an ordinary port of call for passenger steamers. In 1910, even the coaling depot was moved to Byng Inlet on Georgian Bay. 1927 brought the closing of the railway station. Today Algoma Mills is predominantly a residential and resort community. Only the abandoned hotel foundation survives, a reminder of the dream.

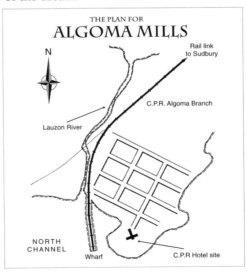

THE PLAN FOR
ALGOMA MILLS

BLIND RIVER

First Mill Fails

Encouraged by the promise of profitable copper deposits, in 1847 the Montreal Mining Company purchased land near the future town of Bruce Mines. The question was where to find milled wood to build the mine and accommodations for the workers. The obvious answer was to use financial incentives to lure a mill operator to this forsaken part of God's earth. Evidently, the incentives were lucrative enough to persuade one Joseph Salvail to relocate his water-powered mill from Lower Canada to Blind River in 1853.

By 1867, *le petit moulin* (the little mill) had grown into a major headache for the mining company. The mill was heading toward financial ruin as a result of a shortage of capital and Salvail's poor managerial skills. Obliged to intervene, the company took over his holdings, including two hundred acres of virgin forest bought from the Mississauga Indians.

The collapse of Blind River's first commercial enterprise was just the beginning of an economic roller coaster that would plague future generations. At its height, the town boasted the largest lumber mill in eastern Canada; at its lowest point, the town was almost bankrupt. In between lies some of the North Channel's most colourful history.

A Feisty Frontier Village

In 1898, Ontario's Premier Arthur Hardy was smiling. He would beat the Americans at their own game. Because of a new American import tax on wood shipped from Canada, the livelihood of many mills along the North Shore was being threatened. To counteract this development, Canada banned the export of logs cut on Crown land to the United States. Cut off from their source of supply, Michigan firms were forced to relocate to the North Shore, thus bringing stability to the region's milling industry for the first time.

Workers at the Eddy Brothers Mill lived in an area nicknamed "Eddyville"

Around 1900 the Michigan-based Morgan Lumber Company purchased the Blind River Lumber Company. It was soon joined by the Eddy Brothers Company which reassembled one of its Bay City, Michigan mills on the western outlet of the Blind River. At the time, the frontier village was characterized by tar paper shacks and cows ambling down muddy streets. Bears were regular visitors but the most common wildlife walked on two legs. Lumberjacks sporting names like "Cruel-Face" McKinnon and "Roaring" Jack Davidson were among the unsavory characters that lined Blind River's underbelly and were shunned by respectable townspeople. Residents had a stringent classification system: "drifters," for example, were all people who did not own chickens and a coop. Even the most affluent, residing on "silk stocking hill" (Lakeside Avenue), erected the requisite hen house whether it was needed or not.

Lumberjacks could choose from one of five watering holes. Their favourite was the Blind River Hotel, better known as the "Bucket of Blood." Each morning before trudging into the bush, the men would wander into a saloon to be served free shots of "courage." Needless to

Local hotels served as watering holes for lumberjacks

say, differences of opinion sometimes occurred and owners relied on the peace-keeping skills of men like Billy La Flamme, whose specialty was removing his peg-leg and bashing reason into brawling parties.

Following Blind River's incorporation in 1906, efforts were made to bring greater civility to the town. Two of the first resolutions that were passed authorized the removal of rotting horse and animal carcasses from the streets and the purchase of handcuffs for use by the new mayor.

Lakeside Avenue, nicknamed " silk stocking hill," with sawdust burner in distance.

However, these resolutions could not address the rash of fires plaguing the town, including one which destroyed much of the Dominion Lumber Company's stock. Who was the arsonist and why was it taking so long to catch him? One can only imagine the collective astonishment and outrage when the perpetrator was finally apprehended: none other than the Fire Chief himself. Apparently a bonus of five dollars was paid for answering each fire call and so the Chief took it upon himself to boost business. During his stay in the Kingston penitentiary, the town purchased a new steam-powered fire engine.

The modern engine was of little help when a devastating blaze completely destroyed the White Pine Lumber Company in 1911, putting 250 men out of work. The water-hose had frozen solidly in the river. The loss of this mill put an end to sixty years of production at the eastern outlet of the Blind River. Only the Eddy Brothers remained as a major mill employer. In 1919 they sold out to J. J. McFadden, who in turn sold to Carpenter-Hixon in 1926.

The new owners began constructing what was to be

the largest lumber mill east of the Rockies. However, euphoria soon turned to despair under the cloud of the Great Depression. In 1930 the mill shut down, reopening for day shifts only from 1933-35. It was a godsend when J. J. McFadden put it back into full production. At the time, sixty-five percent of the town's 2,750 citizens were on relief, and the town had just filed for bankruptcy. The outbreak of war in 1939 saw the beginning of an unprecedented demand for lumber and soon the mill would again turn out record production levels.

The Inferno of 1948

When it was discovered by an aerial mapper in May 1948, the blaze covered a manageable fifteen acres. But like a rampaging monster, it was soon blowing sparks as far as ten miles and blasting smoke 3,500 kilometres (2,000 miles). Plane visibility was affected up to an incredible 8,000 feet. Although no specific cause was ever determined, the results were more than clear. By the time the fire was quelled two months later, 1,000 square miles of forest had been destroyed. That equated to more timber burned than was cut in fifty years of logging.

For fifty cents an hour (and with a threat of imprisonment for non-compliance), more than three thousand men enlisted in the fire-fighting service. Their stories are unforgettable. At Moccasin Lake, Bill Vincent's crew found itself trapped by the blaze. After igniting grass around a pond to create a back fire, Vincent ordered his panicked men to leap into the water. Standing neck deep, they stared so intently at the massive wall of roaring flames that none noticed the terrified black bear who had joined them. At Peshu Lake, the Forest Protection Supervisor Tom Woodside kept the Sault Ste. Marie office informed by telephone as the fire approached. For one chilling moment, as the area around the lake was engulfed, Woodside was heard to shout, "here she comes!" then only the roar of flames. While the team at Peshu Lake fought against odds to beat back the immense fire encroaching on the Ranger Station, the sweat-drenched cook ignored the heat and flames, and continued at his stove. Dinner was on time.

Motivated by the huge acreage losses resulting from the Mississagi fire, a fire at Chapleau and numerous smaller fires, the province encouraged efforts to create artificial rain by seeding the clouds. One such experiment saw pilot "Red" Rodgers drop more than 600 pounds of chemicals from a height of 16,000 feet before running out of oxygen and being forced to land. In its infancy, water bombing was also plagued with difficulty. While virtually stalling the engine over a blazing target, the pilot had to sound a horn as a signal for a crewman to scramble back and push hundreds of water-filled paper bags out of the bomb bay.

Ironically, the smoking carnage set off the boom of the decade at Blind River. *Operation Scorch*, the largest scorched timber salvaging operation in Ontario's history was the result. Since J. J. McFadden had large timber holdings in the burned area, his mill actually profited from the disaster, working at full capacity to process all the salvaged trees.

Uranium: Blessing or Atomic Nightmare?

In 1953 tight-lipped outsiders were seen near Blind River loading and dispatching planes to the north. The group, later nicknamed the "back door staking bee," was involved in a secret mission to lay uranium claims in the region thirty to forty miles northeast of Blind River. In total, more than one thousand claims were made.

Images of a gold rush-type prosperity excited Blind River residents who envisioned the town growing tenfold overnight. Their excitement was quickly dampened when it was decided Blind River was too far away from the mines. Instead, a completely new twentieth-century urban paradise was created near the site. Named Elliot Lake, the new town boasted a hospital, TV station, community centre, shopping plazas, seven schools and even bars decorated with murals.

For Blind River the fallout from this kind of utopian planning proved to be a major drawback. As sociologist Professor Oswald Hall pointed out in Fred Bodsworth's 1961 *Harper's Magazine* article, "Canada's Luxury Ghost Town," such planning rarely makes allowance for a community's less reputable forms of recreation. "These questionable activities are likely to be concentrated in a town on the periphery of the new community; the peripheral town becomes a sort of moral garbage heap."

In truth, nothing had prepared the good citizens of Blind River for this "peripheral" role. In poured booze, bootleggers, and prostitutes (delivered by the busload and replaced every two weeks before they could be recognised by the police). Civil authority broke down. On one occasion, a crowd of two hundred rioted over the arrest of two brawling men, and the mayor and the town's three policemen were pelted with beer bottles.

Within three years, Blind River's population had doubled to five thousand. Dubious about the longevity of the boom, the town council tried to keep a tight rein on the amount of capital spent on expansion. Even so, in 1957 the council members were forced to borrow $50,000 to install a sewer system. This was only the beginning. Despite valiant efforts, by the time the balloon burst, Blind River's debt amounted to $750,000. Then the U. S. Atomic Energy Commission announced that after 1962 it would no longer purchase uranium from the region. The party was over. By 1961 eight of the twelve mines had closed. An ex-Mayor commented with ironic resignation: "it was quite a boom. I hope we don't have another one for quite awhile. It will take a long time to pay for the last one."

Today Blind River is a pleasant, friendly North Channel town which retains at least one legacy of her past, an old brick sawdust burner from McFadden days. It is now part of the veneer-producing mill. The Timber Village Museum is worth a visit to see its displays highlighting the region's lumber trade, the Mississauga Indians, and the history of Blind River.

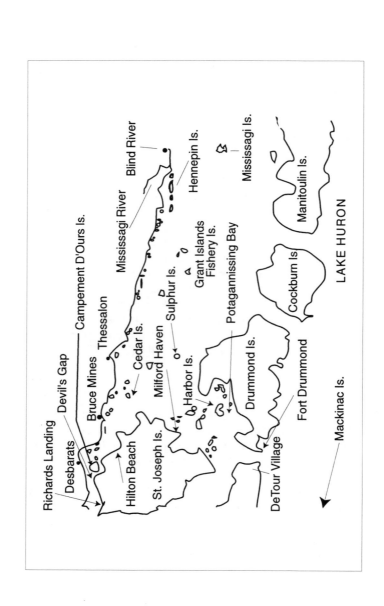

4

WESTERN NORTH CHANNEL

MISSISSAGI RIVER AND ITS DELTA

Fascinating discoveries have been made along the Mississagi River and its delta including Indian campsites from very early nomadic hunters and fishermen; an overgrown graveyard with a tombstone dating to 1836; a forgotten man-made canal; and remains of pioneer dwellings, logging camps and early trading posts. The delta, with its silt-formed islands born of retreating glaciers and their melt waters, is one of the richest sources of human and natural history in the district. It was designated a provincial nature reserve in 1985. A combination of fertile soil and the moderating effects of the North Channel have transformed the delta into a lush paradise of hemlocks, birch, and jack pine, home to many varieties of wildflowers and waterfowl.

The Ojibwe name *Miswezaging*, "river of many mouths," was confusing to Europeans. "Mississagi," a misspelling, is what remains on maps today. In 1640, the Jesuit missionary Father Chaumonot named the local people, *Oumisagi*, which is another name for the Ojibwe tribe we call Mississauga. The river and this land served the people well, providing an abundant supply of sturgeon in the summer, game in winter, and maple sugar in the spring.

The Jesuits were among the first Europeans to settle along the river. In 1670-71, Father Louys André reported that the small Mississagi Mission consisted of a few cabins and a tree stump used for preaching. He commented that "this tribe, in addition to the plurality of wives, and the superstitions that prevail in it . . . is the proudest and most arrogant of all the neighbourhood." Expert in making and using canoes, the Mississauga were destined to become heavily involved in the fur trade which would put its mark on the river nearly 130 years later.

THE HUDSON'S BAY COMPANY TRADING POST

Turbulent Times in Paradise

In 1826, five years after amalgamation with its rival the North West Company, the Hudson's Bay Company considered discontinuing the North West's Mississagi Trading Post. Chief Factor John McBean from neighbouring Fort La Cloche managed to have it spared. He argued that the Mississagi post was key to the interior, particularly to

Temiskaming. Keeping it would send a strong message of the Company's commitment to the region.

Unfortunately, the Mississagi post suffered more than its fair share of headaches. William Cowie, the first factor, drowned with one of his men when their canoe was forced under the ice by a powerful spring current. The next factor, Francis Grant, became mentally deranged and had to be relieved of his duties.

Furs were collected at small outposts like Mississagi.

Over the next few years, the post struggled to survive. In 1845 a curious factor was chosen: Henry Sayer, a rival allied with a competing post. On accepting the job, Sayer convinced the Company to allow him to use his own buildings on the west side of the river rather than those of the HBC post on the east side. Company suspicions were not raised until 1862 when a letter arrived written by a factor named Hopkins. Hopkins claimed that in addition to refurbishing his old buildings, Sayer had also constructed a new store and a men's house: ". . . there is little doubt that the company's hired men have materially assisted in the building, yet Sayer calls them his."

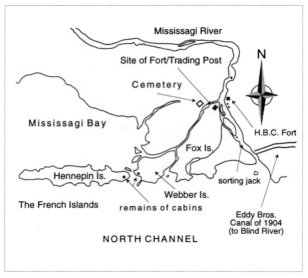

Not surprisingly, the Hudson Bay post did not prosper during his tenure. The chief factor from the Sault agreed that ". . . the company's business appears to be sacrificed to the family interests of Sayer." He counselled, "We cannot lose much by parting with old Sayer, as the trade under the management is very unprofitable

. . . To replace Sayer I can forward you a smart young clerk from hence."

The "smart young clerk," Robert Crawford, stormed up the river, fired Sayer, and confiscated the goods and supplies from his store. Because the site of the first post was now part of the Mississagi Indian Reserve, Crawford had to build at yet another location. He chose Fox Island, a mere stone's throw from Sayer's door. An independent trader once again, Sayer taunted Crawford by selling what the Mississagi Post could not, alcohol. Crawford moaned,

> he intends to deal in whiskey-alcohol. This will be a fearful drawback to us, as our post will be at the centre of an infernal set of grog shops. The Bruce Mines above us, Sayer on the spot and saw mills [Blind River] below.

Despite this formidable competition, the HBC post carried on operations until May 1900, when steady encroachment by Messrs. Eddy and Jordan finally convinced the Company to leave the river to the logging interests.

An Old Era Ends

In the mid-1800s, after most of the timber in the Ottawa Valley and Georgian Bay area had been exhausted, extensive logging began along the North Shore. It was considered a prime location because of the many rivers that flowed into the Channel. Each spring, crews armed with peavies and pike poles broke up the log dumps that had accumulated over the winter at the river's edge, releasing a surge of white pine down the Mississagi River. From May to June, peak black-fly season, the men followed the timber in six-oared boats called "pointers," sleeping in tents at the river's edge. The task of scrambling across the uneven logs to break up logjams was given to the "River hogs" who performed their dangerous work from dawn to dusk despite being soaked by icy waters. Many an unmarked logger's grave lines the banks of the Mississagi.

In 1894, the Mississagi River Improvement Company built a sorting jack at the mouth of the river. Thirty men could run along the floating sidewalks that lined the banks while stamping the logs with the identifying marks of up to eight companies. Then the logs were guided into the appropriate holding pockets. A major breakthrough came in 1904 with the completion of a logging canal to the west branch of the West Blind River. But the back-breaking $18,000 three-mile excavation was soon abandoned because the unpredictable current prevented the logs from actually reaching the mill!

HENNEPIN ISLAND

Hennepin Island was one of many single-family stations that dotted the islands and harbours of the North Channel. Used largely as overnight stopovers, they were modest compared to larger stations with ice facilities and boarding houses where wives and children joined the fishermen during the summer months.

The island's harbour was known as Glanville Harbour.

In 1948, Joseph Glanville had sold his fishing licence to Joseph Brisbois for $750. The deal included a cabin, furniture, machinery, a gas boat and engine (which much to Brisbois' dismay, sank on launching). Confusion came soon after Brisbois built a new dock. He had assumed that the purchase of the fishing licence came with ownership of the land. Not so. Like many fishermen who erected stations on Crown land, Glanville had been a squatter (the government gave fishermen the right to do this). Brisbois abandoned the station, which quickly deteriorated. By 1954 the Ministry of Natural Resources decided that the hazardous building should be removed. However, since the law considered "razing" to be arson, the derelict station had to be torn down board by board.

MISSISSAGI ISLAND LIGHTHOUSE

In order for his daughter Evelyn to be closer to the Blind River school, lightkeeper Foster Morris transferred from Sulphur Island lighthouse to Mississagi in 1928. Education was a struggle for isolated lighthouse children. At the island from April until December, Evelyn was only able to attend school for three months of the year. The rest of the time she had to teach herself from prescribed textbooks. The tenacity and discipline required to do this was learned in part from growing up at a lighthouse. At an age when she was so small she required a chair to reach the coal oil lamp, like many other Canadian lightkeepers' children, Evelyn performed a variety of lighthouse duties. If necessary, she could even take care of the light by herself.

Evelyn's education proceeded smoothly until it was

Like most North Channel lighthouses, Mississagi light was a family place.

time for her to enter high school. In order to gain admission, she would have to write departmental exams. The teacher, however, refused to grant the necessary permission. After Foster Morris complained bitterly to the Board of Education, an inspector was finally sent to assess Evelyn. He was so impressed by her ability that he promised to send lessons to prepare her for the following year's exams. The courses created for Evelyn were the first of their kind in the province, and became the basis for the home study programs still in use throughout Ontario.

The Mississagi light, built in 1884, was tended by Foster Morris for twenty-one years. Struck by lightning in 1949, it burned down and was replaced by a metal tower.

GRANT ISLANDS/FISHERY ISLAND

Beware the Wild Beasts!

Was that bizarre story about wild boar being brought to Fishery Island from Sanford Island near Algoma Mills really true? Apparently so. Arriving on the beach, we found an oddly-shaped, bleached skull with two front tusks. We had heard about earlier plans to establish a game preserve on Sanford Island, abandoned when some of the boar escaped, frightening the neighbouring North Shore residents. Transported to Fishery Island, the boar again had escaped by swimming across to nearby East Grant Island where they gave some unsuspecting sunbathers the shock of their lives. The boar are gone, as is the sizeable fishing station that gave the island its name.

In 1895, Fishery Island was bought by the wealthy lumber and shipping magnate, James Playfair, founder of the Great Lakes Transportation Company which was eventually sold to Canada Steamship Lines. Playfair spent much of his time cruising the Great Lakes. When he lost interest in Fishery Island, it was sold to the American-owned Booth Fisheries. Between 1900 and 1920, Booth controlled much of the lucrative American market and enjoyed a near-monopoly of Great Lakes fishing.

Lying in the middle of the western North Channel and surrounded by shoals, the Grant Islands, East and West, offer a sense of remoteness and peacefulness. They are a contrast one to the other. The more protected Fishery Island has a pebbly beach and is covered with cedar, spruce, and birch, while adjacent East Grant is smooth granite graced by towering pine.

Shipping and lumber tycoon James Playfair (centre,) owner of Fishery Island

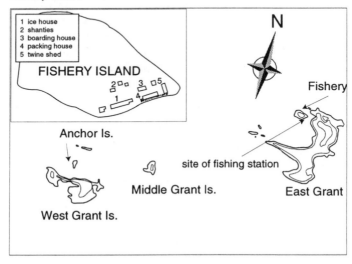

COCKBURN ISLAND

The Forgotten Indian Reserve

From a distance, Cockburn's turn-of-the-century, two-storey houses look like a row of doll's houses standing along the waterfront. This is an authentic, island community of affable, generous people who are expert story-tellers.

Long-time resident, Jack McQuarrie, gave us a tour of the interior of the island on a sunny, blissful Cockburn day. Abandoned homesteads and other remnants of the past poked out from everywhere. From McCaig's Hill, the highest point on the island, the panoramic view shows fields, once laboriously cleared by farmers of the Scotch Block (named after a group of Scottish immigrants), now slowly being reclaimed by the relentless forests. We ended our tour at the weathered remains of an Indian village on the southwest end of the island.

Indians moved to the Cockburn Island Reserve some-time after the signing of the 1862 Treaty of Manitoulin which precipitated the move of Manitoulin's Indian popu-lation onto reserves. Of all the early families, the name Wagosh is still the most strongly attached to the small Indian village. Two Wagoshs were chiefs, and a third became a southpaw pitcher for the Chicago White Sox.

For several years, community members earned their liv-ing working as loggers or as commercial fishermen, but by the turn of the century, most had relocated to Manitoulin Island to a new Cockburn reserve near Shesheguaning so that their children could attend a better school. In 1909, the *Algoma Advocate* was already reporting that "The reserve is now a silent lonely place." All that remains of the village today are a school and a few grey, shingled houses, slowly weathering in a clearing of gnarled apple trees. Tucked into the cool forest are the worn graves of early settlers.

Cockburn Island First Nation, 1920. L to r: Steve Wagosh, Joe Wagosh, Ed Sagon, Bill Wagosh, Louise Wagosh, Agnes Wagosh, Peter Wagosh, George Wagosh

Tolsma: The King of Cockburn

Around 1877, Michigan native, Siberon Falcott Tolsma, chose Cockburn Island as a suitable base for an extensive North Channel fishery. By 1883, his little fishing empire consisted of a 220-foot wharf and a cluster of seventeen buildings. Tolsma was the boss, mayor, and landlord of? Tolsmaville! No one challenged his authority. No one, that is, until William Mundy landed at the wharf.

According to J.E. MacDonald's *Yonder Our Island*, Mundy was a recent immigrant from England who had learned the fishing trade in Little Current before deciding to strike out on his own. A conflict soon developed between Tolsma and Mundy, either because the cocky Mundy criticized Tolma's treatment of his employees, or because Tolsma objected to Mundy's suggestion that he might like to stay in Cockburn. Evidently Tolsma told Mundy to get off his property and Mundy retorted, "I'll go if you're man enough to make me."

The outcome is legendary. As Mundy was the smaller of the two men, everyone expected Tolsma to win the fight easily. Instead, he was rather abruptly knocked to the ground. Tolsma sprang to his feet and thrashed out at Mundy. Next thing he knew he was splayed out on the dock. Red-faced, he pulled himself up yet again, attacking Mundy with fury. Another strong punch and Tolsma was flat on his back for the third time. Humiliated, Tolsma called a truce and shook Mundy's hand. How was he to know that Mundy had been a boxer in the Royal Navy? Despite this introduction, Mundy opted to stay and take up farming.

The Era of Farming and Lumbering

Tolsma's "reign" came to an end when farming and lumbering replaced fishing as the main occupation. After 1878, settlers began to arrive, seduced by land offered at fifty cents an acre. By the late 1800s, 250 people had set up homesteads on Cockburn. One farmer arrived after seeing a two-hundred-pound pumpkin at the Sault Ste.

Marie fair with a tag reading Cockburn Island. Any place that could create such gargantuan produce must surely be another Eden. In the beginning, it was. Cockburn's climate was conducive to growing a wide variety of fruits and to producing fine crops of oats and mixed vegetables. The island also offered excellent grazing land for cattle and sheep. But the farmers soon realized to their dismay that underneath the thin layer of good soil there was only stony, glacial till. By the turn of the century, many had given up and moved on. The remaining families managed a modest living selling produce locally and supplying beef to the lumber operations.

The lumber firm Hitchcock and Foster of Chicago established headquarters in Tolsmaville around 1884. Four 75-man camps and one smaller camp kept the company schooners busy delivering wood to their Drummond Island mill at Johnswood. A few independent jobbers also eked out a living. Periodically they would come into Tolsmaville to replenish their supplies. *Yonder Our Island* recounts the story of one lumberjack who imbibed a little too heavily and, in his exuberance, managed to damage some property. Assistant Constable, Neil McKay, grabbed his handcuffs and handgun and marched into the woods. There would be none of that kind of behaviour in his village! A full day passed . . . no Constable. Fearing the worst, a posse was sent out. Swinging open the door to the lumberjack's cabin, they found the lawmaker and his "prisoner" drunkenly trying to play cards.

Except for an occasional visit, Cockburn had no priest or doctor. Both were needed in Cockburn's 1881 diphtheria epidemic when the community lost many of its residents. Family members had to bury their own dead in

order to protect others from contamination. A few of the
men became quite expert at bone-setting while the island's
women served as medics. J. E. MacDonald writes of Mrs.
John McKay's grandmother, Kitty McKay, who "was a
large woman and very strong. They say that she would go
to the store and put a hundred pound bag of flour on her
shoulder and carry it home." She was often called upon to
deliver island babies. Her fee for this service? A strength-
ening "Toddy."

McKay's fishery, 1906

In isolated communities, travelling clergymen were
often welcome. An Anglican priest, Reverend P. T. Rowe,
described his 1881 trip to Cockburn in the "Algoma
Missionary News". After travelling several days over the
frozen North Channel with dog and sled, he and his com-
panion arrived at the reserve: "The wigwam was pretty
well filled with men, women, children and dogs, still after
a little clearance, I found space enough to stretch myself
by the fire . . . After tea I had a short service among them
and an address. There are only eight families here, and all

living on a reservation of 1800 acres, and are Roman Catholics. I extracted two teeth of a woman who had been suffering several weeks . . ." The following day he held a service for the residents of Tolsmaville. "Every family on the island was represented but four, I was told . . . As I spoke of the Saviour's love in seeking lost sinners, tears flowed down many a sunburned face."

Cockburn Island's winter isolation, 1904

Other ministers were not so eagerly received. A former resident Irene Jones recalled in *Cockburn Island Centennial Paper*, "Many strange events happened but the most gruesome of all was the murder of Rev. Butler whose body was found on the beach with a slashed throat." The murder was never solved, although Cockburn residents have plenty of theories.

Because of their location, people on Cockburn had to make their own fun. Among their favourite activities were square dances played by toe-tapping fiddlers, box socials and even a sock darning contest, judged on speed and the quality of stitches. After a winter of isolation, women eagerly awaited the arrival of a milliner, who set up shop in the boarding house. With great excitement the women would choose their hat from the colourful display spread out on the milliner's bed.

For years, Cockburn struggled without success to get its own lumber mill. A glut of struggling North Channel mills made it difficult for the village to entice an operator. And the lumber company, Hitchcock and Foster, had a cutting monopoly on the island and sent logs to their mill on Drummond Island. Finally, in 1889, the community proposed to build a municipally-operated mill. Naturally, the project was immediately challenged by Hitchcock and Foster. The dispute ended up in a Toronto court where the judge ruled in favour of the lumber company.

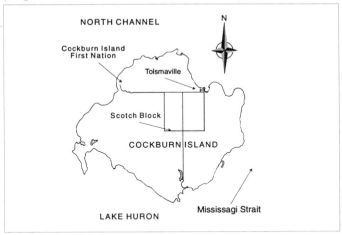

The situation did not change until after new provincial legislation was passed. The law ended the export of Canadian raw timber to the U.S. for milling, effectively stopping H & F's export of Cockburn wood to

Drummond Island. Enticed by a ten-year tax exemption in 1898, George Mackenzie of Thessalon agreed to open a mill on the west side of Tolsma Bay. About the same time, H & F began phasing out its Cockburn operation, possibly because of the tragic death of its manager George Avis (see Sulphur Island p.159).

The village reached its peak between 1900-20. 1914 was a milestone. A telephone cable was laid from the lighthouse at Mississagi Strait across to Cockburn's post office. However, in 1928, the village suffered a terrific blow when its larger mill burned. The Great Depression struck soon after, and Tolsmaville slipped into a vortex of decline as people left in search of work. More would leave during World War II; many never returned. Major economic changes were taking place. Fishing and lumbering had died out and, with a much-improved road system, trucks were threatening to replace ships as the most efficient method of transportation. Cockburn seemed destined to become a ghost town. Today the village has become a summer haven.

THE *TURRET CROWN* AND THE *AGGIE B. REID*

While all shipwrecks are tragic, in hindsight some have a humorous side. Such was the wreck of the *Turret Crown*, a 1,150 ton freighter. In the midst of a thick November snowstorm, the captain stationed a man at the bow to test the depth with a lead line. He was reassured to hear the man confidently shouting, "Lots o' water Cap'! Keep goin' lots o' water Cap'!" Suddenly there was dead silence, followed by a frantic, "Back 'er up Cap'. I just threw the lead line in the bush." There sat the Turret Crown, her bow high and dry on Cockburn Island. Cockburn Island was also the site where the tug *Aggie B. Reid* caught fire. With considerable difficulty, Mr. Reid and his son Frank managed to free the lifeboat. As they desperately rowed away, the blazing vessel chased after them, seemingly possessed by demons.

SULPHUR ISLAND LIGHTHOUSE

Lost on the Ice - February 1898

What a strange sight. As the morning light tinged pink the ice and snowdrifts, a lone sleigh stood in the middle of the frozen North Channel. It was heavily laden with supplies, but no horses or people were visible. Slowly there was a stirring under the snow-covered fur robes and George Avis and teamster Paddy Berry emerged.

They had been on their way from Thessalon to the company store and lumber camps on Cockburn Island, when midway across the twenty-five mile stretch of ice they were caught in a sudden, blinding snowstorm. Realizing they had no compass, Paddy halted the sleigh. He wanted to avoid the possibly fatal mistake of exhausting the animals by travelling aimlessly in circles. The men hunkered down beneath the blankets. The following day, with the maelstrom showing no signs of letting up, Paddy released the horses. For the numb and shivering men there was only one choice: stay under cover until the storm abated.

On the third day, they stared out at the bleak horizon and listened to the sound of cracking ice. Hungry and exhausted, they knew that in order to survive, they had to

Sulphur Island lighthouse destroyed 1968

reach Sulphur Island lighthouse, three miles away. Crawling on elbows and knees, as their hands and feet were severely frozen, the men took most of the day to reach the island. They almost cried when they realized they would have to overcome one last hurdle: a wide moat of knee-deep slush.

The soaked men broke into the lighthouse where they scrounged up some flour, oats, and tea. So weakened from exposure, it took six days before one of them could gather up the strength to climb the 43-ft. (13 m) lighttower. Placing the oil lamp in a sack, and carrying it in his teeth, it took him two hours to struggle up the steep stairs. To their utter dismay, the signal was washed away in the cold brilliance of a full moon.

Luck had not deserted them entirely. The following evening, quite by accident, they were discovered by a Mr. Harper who told them that most people had given up hope of retrieving their bodies before spring. That night when

Harper lit the light, Sulphur's beam was seen in distant Thessalon and a search party was dispatched. The men had been missing nine days. Upon learning of the miraculous rescue, Avis's wife and son rushed from Cockburn Island to Thessalon. Sadly after three days of care and steady improvement, Avis suddenly became delirious and died. Mrs. Avis arrived only to find she had lost her husband for a second time.

The lighthouse on Sulphur Island was built in 1896, and rebuilt in 1903. Following automation, repeated vandalism led to its demolition in 1968.

MILFORD HAVEN

Major Rains, the Educated Polygamist

In June 1848, the eminent biologist, Louis Agassiz, and his research team were en route to Lake Superior when a storm forced them to land on St. Joseph Island. As they pulled up their canoes, Agassiz was approached by an unshaven, dishevelled man who introduced himself as Major William Kingdom Rains.

Agassiz accompanied the stranger to his crude dwelling and was utterly astonished to find a wall-to-wall library including classical volumes in French, Italian and Greek. His host spoke poetically and passionately about politics, science and literature and flattered Agassiz by speaking knowledgeably about his lectures. The rumpled Major then brought out a portrait of himself dressed in full British Army regalia, and grinned as he admitted he had been considered the best-dressed man in the regiment. The scientist was flabbergasted. How did a man of such learning and position come to live here?

Tired of the military, Major Rains had retired at the age of 36. In 1830, accompanied by Frances Doubleday and her sister Eliza, he had sailed for Canada, leaving his estranged wife in England. The three settled on Lake Simcoe until Major Rains could obtain a charter to colonize St. Joseph Island. Full of optimism, Rains and a few other founding families arrived at St. Joseph in 1835. In anticipation of an influx of settlers from England, drawn by a limited offer of 200 acres for each of 100 families, they immediately erected a store and sawmill. To their disappointment, few settlers came to the newly-named Milford Haven. Rains lost a fortune through bad investments and suffered a falling out with his Milford haven partners.

Major Rains gained notoriety for siring 25 children with two sisters.

Rains, his common-law wife Frances, and her sister Eliza relocated for a time to what is now called Rains Point. Whether they felt that the region could not produce a suitably-educated and aristocratic match for Eliza, or whether Rains and Eliza also fell in love is not clear. What is clear, is that between them, Frances and Eliza bore twenty-five of Rains' children, and from all accounts, the families were perfectly content with the arrangement. Many of the children became well-known and respected throughout the area for their various enterprises.

DRUMMOND ISLAND: POTAGANNISSING BAY

First Permanent Female Settler, Betsy Seaman

Late one night in November 1863, Betsy Seaman tossed another log on the fire, and settled wearily into her rocking chair. Her mind was racing. How was she going to clothe and feed eleven children without the support of her husband Daniel whom she had buried earlier that day?

Betsy had married widower Daniel Murray Seaman in 1841, becoming mother to his three children. As her husband was a Mormon, Betsy found herself attached to a new, little-understood religion during its most tumultuous period. Because of its beliefs, especially those surrounding the controversial issue of polygamy, the Mormon colony had been persecuted and driven out of Ohio and Missouri. Followers had been attacked, their farms razed and their women raped. They hoped a move to Nauvoo, Illinois would bring them peace and security but they were to be disappointed. Their founder Joseph Smith was murdered by a mob in 1844 and the church split into factions. The charismatic Brigham Young led his followers to Utah, while a group led by the rebel, James Jesse Strang, eventually settled at Beaver Island in Lake Michigan.

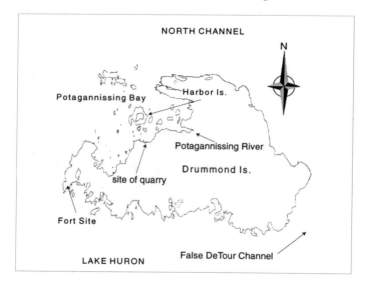

In 1850, the Seamans, who now had six children, joined the three hundred-strong Strangite colony. Wearing a crimson robe and silver crown, Strang had crowned himself King of Beaver Island. He began to actively promote polygamy (an abhorrent concept to Seaman) and enforced penalties of whippings for non-adherence to strict tithing laws and dress codes. When word reached the U.S. government that Strang believed God had given all the islands of the Great Lakes to him, President Millard Fillmore decided it was time to act. He ordered a ship be sent to Beaver Island to bring the self-appointed imperialist and his high-ranking "courtiers" to Detroit where they were charged with everything from murder to treason. To everyone's amazement, after conducting an eloquent defence, Strang and all the defendants were only charged with counterfeiting, mail robbery, trespassing and cutting wood on federal land.

Disillusioned, the Seamans left Beaver Island for Manitoulin around 1853. While anchored in Mackinac Harbor, marauders posing as custom agents raided their schooner and hauled Daniel Seaman ashore. They shredded the sails and cut the stays and rigging. Years later, one of Daniel's sons still harboured vague memories of the horror of waking up to discover his father lashed to the mast as they drifted aimlessly at sea. Later the family moved to Drummond Island.

Kathryne Belden Ashley's *Islands of the Manitou* makes a convincing argument that Seaman and Strang had plans for a new Strangite colony on Drummond Island, but were unable to attract enough Mormon settlers. In 1856, Strang was murdered by two of his disgruntled followers. They had had enough of his despotic rule. Shortly thereafter the residents of Beaver and Mackinac Islands drove out the leaderless colony. In 1980, visitors from Grand Rapids uncovered a cache of coins and paper currency in the vicinity of Strang's former residence on Beaver Island. To this day, other treasure hunters continue to scour the area for money and loot said to have been abandoned in the colonists' hasty departure.

Despite her initial despair at the death of her husband, Betsy Seaman was a survivor. She hired Indians to help her

Daniel Seaman

older boys supply wood to a local fuel depot; and she put her six and eight year olds in charge of scything wild hay along the Potagannissing River for the cattle she began to raise. Before she died at age seventy-five, she had become a much admired figure in the community. The Seamans' portraits hang in the Drummond Island Historical Museum, along with other interesting mementos of the Island's past. Across the road, in the Betsy Seaman Memorial Park, is a plaque commemorating this industrious and resilient pioneer.

DRUMMOND ISLAND QUARRY

In 1853, the same year the Seaman family arrived at Drummond Island, sixty tons of limestone were shipped from a quarry in Potagannissing Bay to Sault Ste. Marie for use in the construction of its first lock. This led the Superintendent of the Drummond Island Stone Quarrying Company, Thomas Stringer, to report enthusiastically to investors that the future was bright for the quarry with its high-quality stone.

Lock construction at the Sault was under the direction of twenty-four-year-old Charles Thompson Harvey. Called "the Greatest Engineer" and "Young Mr. Big" by his biographers, Harvey was an exceptional salesman and promoter, filled with lofty ideas. But his lack of experience would haunt the lock for years. According to Ernest Rankin's "Canalside Superintendent"(*Inland Seas* 1965), the difficulties began when Captain Canfield of the Topographical Corps of Engineers challenged as unsound Harvey's method of building the lock by lining the sides with earth and loose blocks. Canfield's judgement was vindicated when the canal embankments proved to be unstable from the beginning. Superintendent Stringer took little notice of the infighting until Harvey declared the stone from Stringer's Drummond Island quarry inferior, and announced that future contracts were terminated. One can imagine the gloom hanging over the Drummond Island quarry as the scows of limestone from Marblehead on Lake Erie headed past their island to the Sault. The joke would be on Harvey though. The Marblehead stone had been cut from an underwater quarry and when these porous, waterlogged blocks froze, they shattered into thousands of dollars worth of useless rubble.

Prodded into action over concerns about slow progress, the lock's promoters appointed J. W. Brooks to take over the project. Soon, the Drummond Island quarry was back in business. When the State Lock was finally completed in

May 1855, 70,000 tons of Drummond Island limestone had been used. With contracts assured for the next two locks, the company built a 1,000-ft. rock and gravel causeway out into Potagannissing Bay, complete with a railway and a massive loading dock. Drummond Island Yacht Haven was built over the ruins of this causeway.

HARBOR ISLAND

Horseshoe-shaped Harbor Island provides a pleasant retreat from the busy marina at nearby Drummond Island. Today it is uninhabited, but a grassy clearing west of the harbour mouth marks the spot where Jesse Wells Church (1838-1911) and his family lived in their two-storey house. A Renaissance man, Church had varied interests and careers, ranging from master boat builder to doctor. One of the most educated men in the region, Church wrote articles for *Scientific American*; was architect of his father's home on Sugar Island and designed and constructed boats. His journals are filled with meticulous drawings of ships, buildings and other innovative projects.

In the late 1840s, Jesse moved with his family from the Sault to Sugar Island. His enterprising father, Philetus Church, started a successful wood-fuelling depot, shipyard, sawmill and store, selling everything from maple sugar to ornamental trees. He employed native labourers from the Garden River Reserve to chop wood, and to pick blueberries and raspberries for shipment to American mining towns. The Churchs had an Ojibwe maid named

Rosalie La Sarge who captured the heart of their son Jesse. When his strict Presbyterian parents learned that Rosalie was pregnant, Jesse was unceremoniously shipped off to school. But not before he promised to come back for her. Three years later he returned, meeting his son George for the first time. After Jesse and Rosalie were married, the family moved to Traverse City. In the 1860s they returned to the St. Mary's River and built a house on Harbor Island. Here Rosalie gave birth to another six children.

R to l: Phil Church, Jesse Church, Ala May Sutago, Sine Richards, Rosalie Church, Jesse Church Jr.

Although Jesse was occupied with boat-building commissions and tending to the sick, he was never too busy to help others. Hearing that an elderly native woman, Mrs. Buzwah, was to be sent to the poor house in the Sault, he took her in and gave her a small house. Mrs. Buzwah remained a valued member of the family and at one point helped Rosalie perform a clandestine baptism.

The last baby to be born at Harbor Island was Jennylee Church, Rosalie and Jesse's granddaughter. Her Scottish mother, Maggie, loathed Catholics and refused to have Jennylee baptized, much to the distress of the devout Rosalie. One evening while Maggie was sleeping, Rosalie and Mrs. Buzwah, by now blind and crippled, stealthily crept to the Church home and together performed the baby's baptism.

One of the miniature wooden models that Jesse used in his construction business is on display at the Drummond Island Historical Museum. The house he designed for his father on Sugar Island is listed in the National Register of Historic Places. Harbor Island is part of the Nature Conservancy and is a National Wildlife Refuge home to fox, lynx and deer and an important stopover for migratory birds. The Island is open for swimming and exploring (there are no trails) but overnight camping and fires are not permitted.

THESSALON

A Procession of Mills

Thessalon was called *Nayashewan*, "Long Point" by the Indians who had fished and camped here for centuries. Around 1872, a boat laden with Nathaniel Dyment's steam-powered sawmill landed at a spot east of the Thessalon River. According to J. E. MacDonald's *This Point of Land*, a Scotsman hired as a mover eyed the location and inquired, "Mon, Mon, what can ye want wi' a place like this?"

Sorting logs, Thessalon river

Dyment informed him that he was admiring the future site of a mill, to which the Scotsman replied, "Weel, ye're either daft or a bra' mon to ha'e such an idea."

Far from daft, Nathaniel Dyment was not only the founder of a successful venture; but also of a thriving town called Thessalon Mills. All was going well until the mill caught fire in September 1888. The village and lumberyard were spared but neighbouring homesteads were less fortunate. Many families suffered total losses and heavy smoke delayed shipping and train travel. Undaunted, Dyment rebuilt the mill with modern equipment and reaped the rewards of increased productivity.

In 1892, Dyment's twenty-two-year-old son, Albert, took over operations. This freed Nathaniel to concentrate on one of his passions: horse racing. In 1903, his horse, "Thessalon," won the coveted King's Plate in Toronto. In spite of Albert's youth, the mill flourished and Thessalon entered an era of prosperity. A steam-powered woollen mill that did a thriving business in blankets, Mackinaw garments and yarn was established in 1897 and a second lumber mill, owned by the Burtis Mills Company arrived in 1903. To round out its economic base, Thessalon had become a fishing centre.

But the year 1906 marked the beginning of the town's run of bad fortune. The Dyment mill was sold and moved to Nestorville. Unable to engage enough farmers in sheep raising, the woollen factory had to close in 1910. After the Burtis mill was destroyed by fire in 1912, the next casualties came in the 1930s: the Box factory, Asam Basket factory, and others.

Thessalon's Lively Characters

Today Thessalon is a pleasant town, its marina full of yachts bobbing alongside a few commercial fishing boats. The "rough and tumble" feeling of its early lumbering days is gone but the town's old timers (some of whom are proud members of the exclusive "Wait'n for God Club") can spin tales that recreate the picture of Thessalon as a legendary sawmill town full of scamps and scalawags—like Tom Frost.

Tom and his family were squatters in a small house perched on the tiny, rocky island just outside the marina. To get back and forth to town, they used floating logs chained end to end. Tom would sit playing a one-string banjo on his front porch, while simultaneously cutting firewood with a saw bolted to the side of his rocking chair. Often when he was in town, he would offer fruit or vegetables to anyone he met. Very generous, except everyone knew the produce had been liberated from their gardens. Mischievously, Frost would mutter, "The god-damned potatoes aren't doing very good this year! I was at seven of my gardens and none of the potatoes are any good!"

Brawling was common among the surly lumberjacks who sauntered into town to wet their whistles and let off steam. A story is told about two of them who moved onto the street to settle their differences. One of the men complained that there was not enough room for the fight and so, with brute strength, he moved a wagon full of lumber. By the time he turned back his incredulous opponent had fled into woods.

But no one held a candle to Thessalon's town drunk, Walter Clarke, who put a stone through someone's front window every fall to ensure himself a warm place in jail each winter.

Winter seemed to affect everyone in Thessalon. At least every hockey fan. Ken McColman recalls going to Blind River in 1939 for a game: "We got all the guys from the mill and we were going to "clean out" Blind River. 125 men all in trucks. Someone must have called Blind River because they called the game off."

View of Thessalon Woollen mill (centre back). One twelve year old earned 50 cents a day folding blankets and spinning yarn.

Rumours abound that during Prohibition a few of Thessalon's citizens were not above participating in the illicit liquor trade. It is said that there was even an underground tunnel to transport it. After delivery to locations such as Green Island in the Mississagi Strait, American rum-runners would pick it up in high-speed boats. Ken McColman remembers being invited for a ride in a Chris-Craft launch powered by three engines,

> There were only little ripples on the water five or six inches high when he wound that thing up to seventy miles an hour. I thought the bottom was going to come out of that thing. Oh man! I was actually scared. He came back to the dock and loaded everything for DeTour. A Taxi driver brought the booze down. A lot of rum. Americans had a fancy for rum.

Inevitably he was caught by Customs officers who chased him across the water, demanding he stop or be shot. When he ignored the warning, they fired across his bow (which was lined with steel plates for just such an eventuality). He was finally cornered by other patrol boats and sat out the rest of Prohibition in jail.

THE THESSALON LIGHTHOUSE

Many residents still fondly recall Mrs. Harvey, "the brave little lady of the light," who retired as keeper in 1940. Her husband, James, had been appointed the first keeper in 1898 and following his death in 1915, Esther Harvey took over for twenty-five years. She was a great favourite of the local children who used to race each other to the lighthouse to see which one would win the job of delivering her flour and oil. The lucky one would earn the princely sum of five cents.

On the way to the former lighthouse, the children passed several unmarked graves. No one knew for sure who is interred there, but Thessalon resident Ron Showan recalls being told that a steamer had let off a family of settlers—parents with two children. As they rowed to Thessalon, their boat capsized and, in the manner of the day, they were buried where they were found. Showan remembers that no matter the prevailing mood, anyone passing by the mossy mounds would observe a respectful silence.

After the lighthouse was automated in 1952, it was vandalized and later torn down around 1969.

STRANDED ON CEDAR ISLAND

Twenty adventure-packed years salvaging shipwrecks in the North Channel and along the Canadian shore of Lake Superior. Delivering coal in late Fall and hauling logs in winter storms. Still, Thessalon's Ken "Haywire" McColman considers a boyhood adventure on Cedar Island one of his most vivid memories.

On a hot summer day in 1936, twelve-year-old Ken, his sister Ardell and a friend set out for an enjoyable row. As they rounded Thessalon Point, the water turned choppy. Before they could turn back, one of their oars snapped. They tried to paddle, but could not keep control. Finally they gave up and let the boat drift. Within hours, the angry black clouds had grown into a full-blown storm.

Waves sloshed in over the tossing bow. Ken now laughs, "My sister was scared so bad! She was sitting on the bottom of the boat, and bailing over her legs instead of throwing it over the side of the boat!"

Back in Thessalon, their father was sick with worry. He wanted to head out to look for them, but knew a search would be futile. Meanwhile, the drenched and shivering trio landed at about four in the morning on Cedar Island.

At dawn, the storm was still raging. No one would volunteer to start the search with the children's father, no one but their uncle. Travelling west, in the direction of the wind, they peered through the wheelhouse window for any sign of the boat or its occupants. On Cedar Island, although the children could see the McColman tug slowly rising and falling in the swells, nothing they did could get their father's attention. They attempted to sleep but their imaginations played tricks on them. Ken recalls, "As kids you see these rocks out in the water, and they seem to be moving, and we thought sure as hell something out there was trying to get us."

The third day was blessedly calm. As he searched the nearby islands, McColman feared the worst. Again the children watched helplessly as the tug passed by. Finally driven by hunger, they waded into the lake, raised their small boat and bailed it dry. Ken calculated that the wind direction should deliver them to the mainland and off they drifted. They landed near Nestorville and walked to the highway where they were picked up by a man who offered his bag lunch to the famished children. It was gone in the blink of an eye. Ken still laughs thinking of his father's reaction as he and his sister arrived wearily on the doorstep, "He gave us hell!"

BRUCE MINES

In The Beginning

Even though John Keating, Indian Agent for St. Joseph Island, doubted the Indian's story about a massive copper deposit on the North Shore, he felt compelled to investigate. He was very glad he did. In the summer of 1846, he struck a bonanza: black bedrock laced with gleaming veins of white quartzite, run through with rich deposits of copper minerals.

His timing, though, could not have been worse. Prospecting fever was sweeping Ontario and the government was so flooded with speculators clamouring for mining permits that it shut its doors to catch up on the paperwork. Keating was one of the last to obtain a permit and,

Early Bruce Mines

to his horror, discovered that it had mistakenly been issued for an inferior parcel of land. With the office closed, his only option was to buy the valuable land outright. Not an easy task for a man as poor as William Keating.

He contacted Arthur Rankin, a former associate in Windsor, but even their combined resources fell short. Then they approached James Cuthbertson, a wealthy Montreal merchant with a penchant for mining ventures. In July of 1847, their mine, named after James Bruce, the newly-appointed Governor General of Canada, sent its first shipment of ore by schooner to Boston: two hundred tons of copper.

Shortly after this first shipment, Cuthbertson sold his shares to the Montreal Mining Company. The land containing the rich ore was held in his name alone, and he made a fortune. Keating and Rankin stayed at Bruce Mines and struggled with minimal success to make a go of their property.

The First Copper Mining Town in Canada

In the 1850s, exhausted tin and copper mines in England put a quarter of a million miners out of work. Desperately seeking a new start, they sailed for Canada, the United States, South Africa, Cuba and Spain, anywhere they could wield their pickaxes. For most of them, mining was all they knew.

These miners were familiar with back-breaking labour, but at Bruce Mines they also had to face being separated from their families. About seventy Cornish miners, nicknamed "Cousin Jacks," carved a "bachelor village" out of the wilderness. Some lived in a dozen crude windowless

*The first miners at Bruce Mines were immigrants from Cornwall,
England.*

cabins with dirt floors, while others set up canvas tents. In 1848, they began to tunnel underground with hand tools and explosives, the darkness lit only by tallow candles attached to their felt hats.

Over the next three years, offices, stores, warehouses, and wharves were built even though the Montreal Mining Company was on shaky financial ground. The cost of preparing the ore was too high and so the company decided to buy an expensive ore-dressing machine, a copper smelter and a refiner. The smelter promptly went up in flames and the company had to act swiftly to soothe nervous shareholders. They took miners off the "tut system," which paid according to the amount of ground cut and initiated the "tribute system" which paid according to the amount of high-quality ore removed. Productivity shot up, but so did the danger of having too many tunnels open as miners worked only the more promising veins.

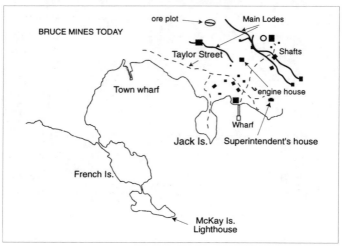

In 1853, the Montreal Mining Company, in need of funds, leased a portion of its land to the West Canada Mining Company (WCM Co.). Fate smiled on the new owners when a cow belonging to miner-farmer, George Clark, strayed on to their property and slipped on a piece of charred moss. The vein of copper that was accidentally exposed turned out to be a bonanza for the company, turning it into one of the world's leading copper producers. Clark's reward for his part in the discovery of the "fire load" was a barrel of flour.

The WCM Co. hoped to bolster profits at their new Wellington Mine by hiring a mining captain with his eye on the bottom line. In 1861, William Plummer (grandfather of actor Christopher Plummer) announced that miners would lose their half-day holiday on Saturdays and must work a regular twelve-hour day. A riot erupted after hundreds of enraged workers protested unsuccessfully to an unsympathetic management. Company offices were sacked, the general manager's life threatened and an angry mob dumped one hundred barrels of ore valued at $250 a barrel into the harbour. Plummer backed down. These Cornishmen were honest, frugal, hard-working and religious. They could survive being worked to the bone, but taking away their one taste of freedom was the last straw.

A copper miner's day began before the sun came up and ended after it went down. In the oppressively cold mines, he often worked from a small wooden platform driven into a vertical rock face weeping with water. He could see only the few feet of rock directly in front and he was surrounded by the relentless sounds of dripping water, of men chipping rock and an occasional deafening explosion.

One visitor described the mine in 1867,

We descended two of the shafts to the depth of 70 fathoms, and although the day above was excessively hot, we had no sooner gone to the depth of about 30 feet than we came upon perpetual ice. The ladders are almost perpendicular; the descent being broken from time to time by artificial galleries constructed to work out the vein. This vein is 25 feet in width, but I regret to say it becomes poorer the deeper it is worked downwards.

Many of the children of the Cousin Jacks followed their fathers into the mines. John Semen began work at the age of ten. He recalled, "Life was made up of eating and drinking, working and sleeping, a sort of machine existence without poetry, or inspiration." As a child in 1862, when men were paid one dollar per day, he earned sixty cents a day. All his wages were turned over to his mother to help support the family. Once a year, John received fifty cents.

In the 1860s, the shacks of the original Cornish miners had been replaced by frame houses and gardens. The town of 1,500 was an eclectic blend of company officials, hard-working mining families, and characters like William Firmstone, whose long grey beard turned green from working at the smelter. He was a fine complement to the lime-coloured pigs that wallowed in the coppery sludge oozing down the smelter sluice-way into the lake. Another local character was "Elijah the Prophet" who made his predictions standing on a giant pudding stone rock downtown. (The rock was later turned into a monument to WWI soldiers.) Elijah's psychic ability was somewhat suspect until he accurately foretold of the 1863 fire that destroyed most of Bruce Mines. As the blaze approached, people wrapped their treasured possessions in blankets and dropped them into the lake. Churning waves unwound the blankets, strewing their contents along the shore. Even today plate shards occasionally appear.

Bruce Mines was a company town. The Montreal Mining Company owned the property, ran the stores and set the prices. In the fall of 1862, a man named George Marks became the first to challenge the monopoly. As winter approached, Marks sailed his schooner into the harbour, dropped anchor and waited patiently for the ice to form. Management fumed as they helplessly watched the residents stream across to the ship/store.

The following spring the cocky Mr. Marks anchored a scow a few feet from the dock. Customers either waded across or waited until he lowered a drawbridge. Soon unable to resist the temptation, he nailed a ramp to the dock. Almost immediately, an axe-wielding group of company thugs descended on the gangway, only to skulk off when confronted by Marks brandishing a pistol. After this stand-off, Marks was permitted to open a store on property rented from the company. Bruce Mines was officially open to free enterprise.

Main Street Bruce Mines, 1903

In 1864, after buying out the Montreal Mining Company, the West Canada Mining Company saw its profits start to decline. The reasons were identified as: too costly dressing of the ore, too great a loss of copper through washing, and the exorbitant expense of shipping ore to England. Unfortunately a new smelting technique failed to improve ore quality, and the cost of importing salt and scrap iron became prohibitive. The final blow to the once profitable Wellington Mine came on a Saturday night in 1876. Mercifully empty of miners, the mine collapsed. When workers went in to see if any ore could be recovered, they found an underground lake ten feet above the water level of the North Channel. The flooded shaft brought an important chapter in Bruce Mines' history to an end.

With the town's major employer now gone an exodus of wagons piled with belongings began. Over the years, the mines were reopened for short periods but with only marginal success. Some new enterprises did take hold, including an 1897 trap rock quarry which supplied the hard blue-grey rock needed to make strong road surfaces. Today Bruce Mines continues to celebrate its mining heritage. The Bruce Mines Museum and Archives, located in an old Presbyterian Church, displays artifacts from the illustrious mining era as well as military paraphernalia and antiques. For a glimpse into the operation of an early copper mine, visitors can visit the Simpson Shaft with its horse-powered hoisting machine, mining equipment and small mine shaft.

HILTON BEACH

Hill Town, Marksville becomes Hilton Beach

After an unsuccessful day of searching for copper, Major Rains and his son Tudor emerged high on a slope and looked down at a small settlement tucked into the fold of the hills. They called it Hill Town. Among missionaries, it had an unsavoury reputation: " . . . because the Miners from Bruce Mines go there to get drunk, because they can't get liquor at Bruce Mines."

In 1861, John Marks, one of the region's most interesting businessmen, purchased property to build a subdivision. Soon dissatisfied with the economic prospects of Hill Town he next muscled in on Tudor Rains' booming business at Sailors Encampment by setting up a rival store and wood-fuelling dock. After the tragic drowning deaths of his daughter and another child, he returned to Hill Town to open a store, wood-fuelling dock and later a post office, operating under the name "Marksville." Business savvy must have run in the family; around the same time his brother George appeared at Bruce Mines with a schooner/store and single-handedly broke the mining company's mercantile monopoly on the town (see p.183).

The procedure for most early settlers was to arrive at Bruce Mines, purchase land, then hire a small boat to take them across to Marksville. The Young family, however, showed a little foresight by purchasing their land and contracting for a house the year before their arrival. An excellent idea, but one that went slightly awry according to an account in Estelle and Joseph Bayliss' *Historic St. Joseph Island*. As the wharf was not yet attached to the shore, the Youngs with their nine children, oxen and worldly effects had to be ferried ashore—a tedious experience involving many trips back and forth. Finally, after a long, tiring wagon ride they arrived to find their 16 by 24-foot dwelling already occupied by a family with eight children. What to do? The Youngs squeezed themselves into the house and the twenty-one newcomers lived together for nearly three months until the "guests" found new accommodation.

The first hotel on St. Joseph Island was built in 1879 at Marksville by J. Archibald. Eleven years later it was moved and is now part of the Hilton Beach Hotel. In the early 1880s, two mills sprang up at Richards Landing and Marksville. In 1910, the Stone Lumber Company bought the Marksville lumber mill and built a tram line extending out into the lake. Eight miles of railroad track were later added to provide better access to the prime stands of wood on the mountain. The locomotive, rebuilt from a train wreck at Bruce Mines, pulled a string of cars to the far side of the mill where the lumber was dumped in a pond. To meet the heavy demand, both the train and mill operated twenty-four hours a day with the help of about thirty year-round workers. In winter extra men were hired for cutting and skidding logs to the track. Old timers recall how the train stopped at crossings to give right of way, and how everyone for miles around would set their watches by the ever-punctual mill whistle. By 1919, two and a half million board feet of lumber had been cut and shipped as far away as South Africa while the prized birdseye maple was sent to England.

Marksville School, 1908

Ninety-year-old trapper, Jim Reed, remembers the days when Marksville's main street was littered with sawdust. He also recalls the sound of cow bells from fifteen or twenty cows released each morning to graze amongst the buildings and streets. With cows, chickens, goats and geese milling about, a Dr. Lipset became tired of his neighbourhood looking like a perpetual barnyard, not to mention his health concerns. But township law did not allow the community to enforce the tethering and corralling of the animals.

In order to create its own by-laws, the village separated from the township in 1921. In so doing, it took a new name—Hilton Beach. Well, the name wasn't entirely new: there was Hilton Township, a Hilton Road, and for years in Hill Town, there had been Hilton Wharf. Worth a visit is the St. Joseph Island Museum Village located on the I-Line. This six-building complex consists of a two-storey barn, a log cabin, the first school house erected in Sailors Encampment in 1876, a brick schoolhouse, the 1912 Kentvale store and a stone church. Among the intriguing displays are a Hilton Beach fire-truck dating from 1921 and a sleigh-hearse.

DESBARATS AREA

Information for the Desbarats sections is taken from Hermon Dunlap Smith's pamphlet, "The Desbarats Country."

In the late 1800s, many American communities underwent a dramatic transformation, not all of it good. Industrialization had brought economic progress and wealth but also "brain fag," a term coined to describe the stress experienced by urban dwellers of large overcrowded cities suffering under unhealthy environmental conditions.

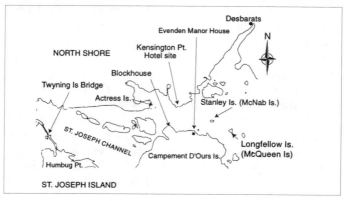

One observer of Pittsburg wrote, "Every street appears to end in a huge black cloud. By day, there is smoke, smoke, smoke—everywhere smoke. By night, it's Hell with the lid off." There was only one prescription: a vacation, preferably a "rest cure in a canoe." Desbarats was one of the chosen destinations. Families would arrive by train or by ship at Hilton Beach or Richards Landing and be ferried to their summer camps along with their servants and trunkloads of "essentials" such as sets of china, suits, corsets, bloomers and evening dresses.

Desbarats was named for George Pascal Desbarats, an entrepreneur with interests in printing, publishing and glass in Vaudreuil, Quebec who was lured to the area by the bonanza copper find at Bruce Mines. In 1847 he purchased mineral rights in Portlock Harbour but allowed the rights to lapse when the site did not prove to be commercially viable.

Today Desbarats refers to the town built up around the Canadian Pacific rail line as well as to the area beginning at the harbour below Portlock Island and encompassing all the islands below the bridge. Rustic summer camps dating back to the turn of the century dot the shores and are still owned by descendants of the original American families (many from Chicago) who first fell in love with Desbarats.

CAMPEMENT D'OURS ISLAND

Dead Man Identified By Pickle Jar

One of the larger islands in the Desbarats area is Campement D'Ours (pronounced "campador"). In May

1867, Campement D'Ours' first resident, James Walker, discovered a corpse in a state of advanced decay along the shore of Doris Island. As he started to move the body, he felt something hard and bulky. In the jacket pocket there was a jar of pickles.

Walker towed the body to Bruce Mines, where an inquest was held. The pickles were used as evidence to connect the body to a missing workman from the limestone quarry on Campement D'Ours Island. Two workmen had evidently returned to the quarry to retrieve their tools. Along the way, one purchased a jar of pickles. After the men parted, he was never seen again. The members of the inquest panel passed the pickles around the room and soberly drew up their findings: drowned through the ice due to carelessness.

According to Edward Capp's *Annals of Sault Ste. Marie*, after the members had agreed on the cause of death, the room fell silent. Every pair of eyes rested on the jar. Finally, someone spoke: "Well fellers, them pickles ain't much the worse for wear, I moves we eat 'em." And without further ado, the jar was opened.

The Flamboyant H. W. Evenden (and Others)

In 1898, a wealthy, flamboyant Englishman, H. W. Evenden, bought Campement D'Ours Island for $4,500 and built the large manor house that still stands opposite Kensington Point. His was the first of several summer residences soon to be constructed at Desbarats. Evenden was the son of a well-to-do draper who fled Britain after a failed marriage to a woman "beneath his station" had caused him to be ostracized by the social elite. In an inter-

view published in the *Eastbourne Gazette* near the turn of
the century, Evenden enthused about the pristine nature of
the St. Mary's River, the healthy climate, the fine fishing
and the ease with which he could flag down a steamer if
freight or guests needed to be transported. He also
described his future plans to raise Himalayan goats on
Campement D'Ours Island and to start a Gruyere cheese
factory.

However, Evenden's expensive lifestyle caught up with
him. In 1902 he sold out to Arnold Scudder who promptly divided the island into lots and set about enticing
wealthy Americans to build summer residences. To attract
tourists, Scudder built the "blockhouse," an exact replica
of one at Fort Mackinac on Lake Michigan. This unique
building was later used as a cottage by the charismatic
Chase Osborn, Governor of Michigan from 1911-1912.
Osborn, a newspaper publisher, writer, prospector, philan-
thropist and political activist, was a welcome addition to
an already vibrant summer community.

In 1913, Scudder sold Evenden's "Manor House" to six
summer residents who set up the "Campement D'Ours
Syndicate" in order to preserve the area as the charming,
unspoiled summer haven they had always known.

LONGFELLOW AND ACTRESS ISLANDS

In 1899, the consummate promoter L. O. Armstrong,
Land and Colonization Agent of the Canadian Pacific
Railway, built a summer home on Stanley Island. So cap-
tivated was he by Desbarats' charm and beauty that he

purchased a further six thousand acres on the mainland. He believed passionately in the area's potential for tourism and was willing to go a long way to realize his dream.

To raise the profile of Desbarats and to bolster its romantic image, he hired a group of Ojibwe to attend the Boston Massachusetts Sportsmen's Show in the winter of 1900. At the same time, he sent the band's chief and community leaders to Cambridge to the home of American poet Henry Wadsworth Longfellow, author of *The Song of Hiawatha*. During their visit, natives presented Longfellow's three daughters with an invitation written on birch bark:

> Ladies: We loved your father. The memory of our people will never die as long as your father's song lives, and that will live forever Will you and your husbands and Miss Longfellow come and see us and stay in our royal wigwams on an island in Hiawatha's playground, in the land of the Ojibways? We want you to see us live over again the life of Hiawatha in his own country.   Kabaoosa
> Wabunosa

The invitation was graciously accepted. In August, a dozen guests were greeted at the Desbarats train station by Indians in full traditional costume. They were ferried by canoe and sailboat to an island known today as Longfellow Island, where they were entertained with native songs, dancing and storytelling. Following this introduction they set out for the "theatre" two miles away on the mainland. Teepees representing an Indian village surrounded the stage, which was built around a tall pine tree. Behind, the ground rose gently to create a natural

Hiawatha *performers from Garden River travelled the U.S. and Europe. A number of children shown here acted the adult roles in a 1960s revival.*

amphitheatre. Because of his high-profile guests, Armstrong had been able to attract the Press. They loved *Hiawatha* and their reviews made it an instant hit. People flocked to see the play giving Armstrong a perfect opportunity to further promote the Desbarats area.

A small scandal arose around Madame Roy who played Minnehaha. Prior to *Hiawatha* her only claim to acting fame had been her portrayal of an Egyptian in *Ben Hur*. Madame Roy had a penchant for wearing coveralls. This unorthodox behaviour was a little ahead of its time and caused such a commotion that the play was boycotted. Stores refused to serve her. The island she lived on has been immortalized as Actress Island.

DEVIL'S GAP

Dwelling Place of Ghosts?

Sometime before the turn of the century, two mailmen, crossing the frozen expanse by dog team, were caught in a snowstorm. Men and dogs quickly became exhausted by the blinding snow and sought shelter at Devil's Gap. The next day a search party spotted them in the distance. The sounds of barking and whimpering filled the air. Yet as the rescuers approached, the crouching figures remained as still as statues. Sadly they had fallen into a hypothermic slumber and froze to death.

Over the years something bizarre occurred. In the exact place where the men had died, two patches of lichen grew taking the form of two men bearing backpacks. It was uncanny. Even sceptics could not deny the shapes were two distinctly human figures. During the summer of 1952, someone took it upon himself to scrape the fungus off the rock to see if it would return in the same shapes. It did not.

ST. JOSEPH ISLAND FERRIES AND BRIDGE

The cable ferry service started by George Langstaff in 1919 gave the islanders a most welcome link to the mainland. A scow equipped with both steam and gasoline power ran along a 2,000-foot cable between Campement D'Ours Island and Kensington Point. The only drawback was the steep hill on Campement D'Ours Island. Resident Jim Reed recalls seeing many a Ford Model T backing up the incline from the ferry. Because the fuel in Model Ts was delivered by gravity to the engine, the gas tank, which in most models was located under the front seat, had to be higher than the carburetor. Thus going up a steep grade in reverse would keep the fuel flowing. (An added benefit was more climbing power because reverse was a lower gear than forward.)

In 1923 Walter Lay won the bid to operate a second cable ferry, *The Magic Carpet,* from Pine Island to the mainland. According to Margaret McKay of Richards Landing, the cable had to be replaced several times owing to the strain put on it by the strong current. She remembers one blustery day when the cable snapped while the ferry was full of travellers and farmers transporting produce and livestock. People watched in horror as the untethered boat was quickly swept down the St. Joseph's Channel. On deck the nervous passengers tried to stay out of the way of a horse, sliding from side to side. Eventually, a tug pulled them to safety.

The bridge committee

In 1934, both ferries were sold to the Ontario Government which initiated free service for passengers and freight. In December 1952, a new diesel-powered ferry, *The Joseph Islander*, was put into service at Humbug Point. Over the years, bridges and causeways were constructed to connect a number of small islands, thus shortening the ferry run. Nevertheless, the islanders still wanted a bridge connection to the mainland.

As far back as 1880, a committee had been struck to lobby for a bridge. It took only ninety-three years for the islanders to get their wish. By that time, tourism had increased to such an extent that often the ferry line-ups were a mile long. The Federal government finally ordered the building of a bridge. To avoid blocking the channel, it was designed to convert into a lift bridge when necessary.

RICHARDS LANDING

John Richard arrived at St. Joseph Island on business and never left. He convinced others to stay to help him build a town, like Elijah Good who was en route to Saskatchewan to start a blacksmith business. As sawmills did not exist, the first homes were made of logs and topped with cedar bark roofs. By the time "Richards Landing" reached its peak in 1878, there was a dock, store and post office all built by Richards.

A vivid picture of what greeted the newcomers is painted in Gregory Lay's booklet *Memories of Early Days on St. Joseph Island*,

Trails were opened up and access was given to

the various concessions .. The swamp roads had
to be crosswayed or corduroyed as the work of
ditching and grading was beyond our means. Before
the roads were finished trees were felled and flat-
tened on top and placed alongside of the road for
the travellers on foot.

Upon their arrival, the original settlers had plenty of
provisions to last the winter. This gave Richard a false
impression of how much stock was needed for his store.
The following winter was long and bitterly cold, and his
shelves were soon bare. The settlers did the best they
could. Some made the dangerous crossing to Bruce Mines
on foot to buy food while others resorted to digging up
their recently-planted potatoes.

Despite the hardships, a strong pioneer spirit encouraged the islanders to co-operate in creating roads and to
participate in logging and building bees. It was immensely
satisfying to watch a community grow. However, a good
sense of humour was essential to survive in such an environment. Gregory Lay recounts the story of a group of
friends returning home from Richards Landing. One
prankster dressed himself in a white sheet and terrified an
unsuspecting settler who was walking along the road.
They laughed for years at the memory of the victim plead-
ing with the "spectre" in the moonlight, "Oh Lord, don't
take me, for I'm an honest man."

By the turn of the century, Richards Landing was a
thriving community and mail centre for the whole island.
It was also an important shipping centre. Produce from
the "garden of Algoma" was so sought after that packet
ships from the Sault would pick it up and deliver it to
other communities. Farmers could also sell directly to

schooners and steamers through such outlets as Tudor Rains' wood-fuelling depot at Sailors Encampment.

Prosperity did not exclude hardship. The winter of 1923 was so severe that blocked roads meant no one could move for months. According to "Island Clippings," a newsletter written by Eleanor Adcock, the village mail carrier, Will Morton, had to teeter along a fifteen-foot snowbank in order to cover his route. He was so elevated, he could see the Rogers family eating supper through the second-storey window above their tinsmith business.

Although the weather could be harsh, even more devastating was the constant threat of fire from wood-burning stoves. First the sawmill burned; then the business section was nearly wiped out in 1907. Fires in 1916, 1922, 1925 and 1937 wreaked havoc on the town. Yet nothing proved as cruel as the Great Depression, closing the doors of many of the remaining businesses. Stubbornly, Richards Landing survived that difficult period and continues to exert its friendly charm, thanks to the loyalty of its citizens.

Main Street Richards Landing c. 1900

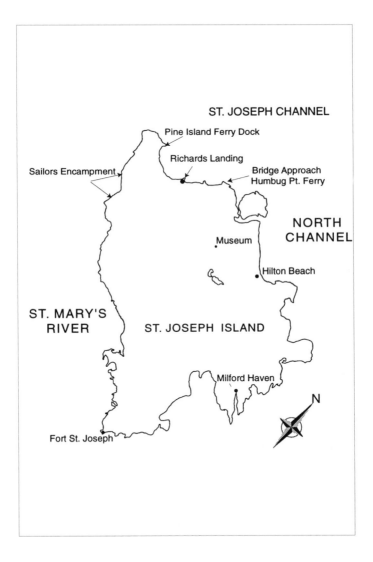

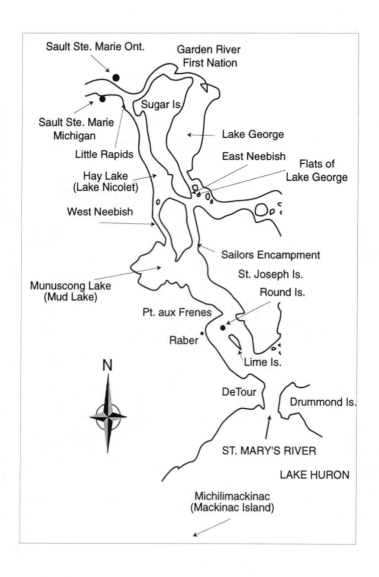

5

ST. MARY'S RIVER

The Big River Family

Technically a 63-mile strait split by Sugar Island, the St. Mary's River is the crucial waterway joining Lakes Huron and Superior. Boating the St. Mary's comes with such ease it is easy to forget the headaches this river once presented shipping. An 1838 article in *Gazetteer of Michigan* suggests the stress of sailing a schooner through the waterway: "The Strait of St. Mary's to the falls is the most difficult to navigate. Its common sailing channel is a perfect labyrinth, devious and circuitous, around islands and sunken rocks, passing across channels and shoals."

The discovery of copper and iron ore on Lake Superior led to the construction of the Michigan State Lock and Canal (completed in 1855), enabling ships to bypass the

21-foot drop of the boiling St. Mary's Rapids. Even with the lock and canal, captains were still tested by the river's obstacles: a limestone bar blocking the entrance into Lake George; Middle Neebish Rapids; and Little Rapids on Lake Nicolet (Hay Lake to locals and sailors) near the northern tip of Sugar Island. When in 1820, Governor Lewis Cass's expedition travelled up Hay Lake on their way to build Fort Brady in Sault Ste. Marie, four of his canoes were damaged trying to navigate these rapids. One of the crew members wrote, "For ten minutes our canoe with all men at oars and paddles did not stir three feet either way."

Under certain conditions, Little Rapids could be traversed from Sugar Island to the mainland. Bernard Arbic's *Sugar Island Sampler* tells how Ed Boulley managed to do this using a team comprised of an ox and horse. His grandson explained, "Grandpa used to have to switch the team around for the return trip to the island, because it worked best to have the ox on the upstream side to hold against the current."

Today, a uniform channel has been dredged and blasted through the River. Lake freighters no longer have any connection with the communities along its banks. In the early days, steamers in search of fuel frequented the many docks stretching out into the river, enabling crews and locals to exchange news and pleasantries. Residents had their favourite captains, captains their favourite locals: experienced pilots who could navigate vessels and cargo safely through the St. Mary's obstacle course.

The river was the lifeblood for both community and commerce. As a result, an interdependence grew between them. Passing ships were part of a "big river family."

Someone wanting to get to the Sault would only have to
row out into the middle of the channel, wait for a sympathetic crew member to toss a line and enjoy a comfortable
tow. Children's summer entertainment included swimming
out, grabbing hold of a trailing line, riding upriver a mile
or two, and then swimming home. In *Inland Seas* Dana
Bowen recounts a captain's stories of the barns built largely from lumber he had "donated." When a barn or house
under construction would come into view, he would hear
the carpenter shouting, "How about a few pieces for the
barn Cap'n! We just run out!" Big hearted, the Captain
would offer up a few planks from the load. In return for
this kind of consideration, concerned citizens like Philetus
Church took it upon themselves to install the first aids to
navigation. From 1865 until 1902, Church ordered his
own tug boat captain to place markers on one section of
the river.

Taming the river turned out to be a monumental task.
From the War of 1812 to the creation of the International
Boundary, the events along the river represent a micro-
cosm of the unfolding relationship between Canada and
the United States. Today the St. Mary's is a river without
borders.

The Big Blockade of 1926

When sailors think of the St. Mary's, many think of the
late Fall of 1926. Lake boats were crammed along the
docks of Port Arthur at the far end of Lake Superior waiting to load their final cargo of grain. Captains paced nervously. It was November 30 and their shipping insurance
was going to expire at midnight. As soon as they were

loaded, twenty-two bulk freighters dashed toward the Sault. Despite their silent prayers, Mother Nature turned against them. As ships began to converge in the St. Mary's River, the thermometer plummeted and thick ice formed rapidly around *Coulee*, a steamer wedged across the rock cut beside Neebish Island. Behind her, sixty ships were blocked and shortly gripped by ice. As the days passed, the channels became more and more congested. At night, the river shimmered as the miles of lights transformed the St. Mary's into a cityscape. During the day, farmers carried on a lucrative business selling fresh milk, beef and sacks of potatoes. Frustrated crews counted the hours. Businessmen fretted over lost income.

Waiting for the ice to break up freeing them to head down the St. Mary's.

Exhausted tugboat crews worked to free the vessels from 4 a.m. until 11 p.m. It was a frustrating job. No sooner would a ship be freed than the ice would imprison it again.

After two weeks the ice-crushing ferry from Michigan finally arrived to open the channel. When the tugs tallied up their work, 149 downbound ships and 98 upbound ships had been freed. For the surviving crew members, the experience was like a badge of honour. When anyone bragged about their ordeals working on the lakes, the sailors would counter, "Oh yeah—but were you sailing December of '26?"

DRUMMOND ISLAND: COLLIER'S HARBOR

A Beleaguered Garrison: Scurvy and Desertion

British Lieutenant Colonel Robert McDouall pulled the blanket over the dead soldier's face, covering his swollen gums and hollow eyes. This was the fifth man lost to scurvy and still there was no response to his urgent request for a shipment of lime juice. Walking home along Promande Street one evening in 1816, McDouall turned a deaf ear to the sounds of drunken revelry drifting from the soldiers' homes. Liquor was strictly prohibited, but his garrison of 350 men was being driven to distraction by an idle life. McDouall was disheartened not only by the outcome of the War of 1812 but also by the poor state of his garrison. In his opinion, the blame lay with his superiors in Quebec and Britain.

His men had helped capture Fort Michilimackinac, (see p.220) and then, in 1814, defended it against American attack. After the Treaty of Ghent restored the fort to the U.S., McDouall was only one of many who wondered if their efforts had been worth the risk. It had been his dilemma to decide where to relocate the garrison. Fort St. Joseph was too dilapidated to reconstruct and there were few suitable alternatives. He finally chose Drummond Island even though the issue of ownership was still in dispute. Until the boundary was settled, he could not proceed with the construction of a fortified post on the north-west summit.

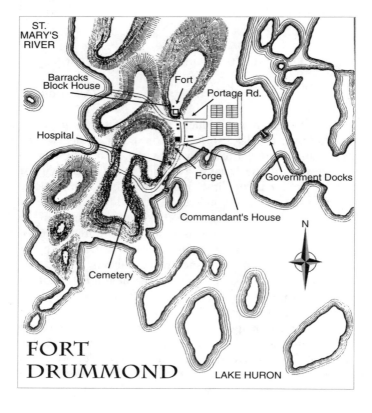

Overgrown graveyard in 1896. Many of the soldiers buried here died from scurvy.

It was, however, the lack of official support for the expensive but essential Indian gift-giving ceremony that most infuriated McDouall. Each year, the British spent as much as $100,000 on gifts of blankets, guns, knives, trade silver and copper kettles for the more than 3,000 natives who camped at Drummond and DeTour. Clearly the government did not sufficiently appreciate the fragility of this post-war period. In the event of another war, unless Britain actively reinforced ties with the Indian nations, she could be left without their support. Yet McDouall's concerns and this strategic northern region were ignored. With a heavy heart McDouall decided to resign.

For twelve years, soldiers, tradesmen, and fur traders shared Drummond Island with a village of Indians, and some other colourful characters, as described in Kathryne Belden Ashley's *Islands of the Manitou*:

The residents included a French nobleman, a dwarf,
and a man without hair on his head or nails on his fingers. Another was tattooed from head to foot with
strange figures. Another man was of the old school and
wore the white, pig-tailed, ribboned wig of days gone
by . . . Drummond Island was a melting pot of French,
Spanish, German, Englishmen, and Indians.

As far as the garrison was apparently concerned, little had
changed since McDouall's departure. John Bigsby, author of
Shoe and the Canoe, wrote in 1823:

The friendly and intelligent gentlemen of the garrison
had little to do save read, hunt for fossils, fish, shoot,
cut down trees, and plant potatoes. Their military
duties took up little of their time . . . I dined at the officers' mess. A small square lump of highly-salted beef, a
fowl (perhaps two), a suet-dumpling, and two dishes of
potatoes, were both dinner and dessert. This was followed by a poor Sicilian wine . . .

Although there were strict regulations against drinking
among the lower ranks, Bigsby reported seeing excessive
drunkenness. Boredom was a good part of the problem. On
one occasion, according to Bigsby, the commandant sent to
Detroit for a group of card sharks, into "whose pockets the
men joyfully poured their money." Bigsby also wrote of the
recurrent problem of desertion which ended so tragically for
five of the garrison.

While I was there, an order came from Quebec to the
post, forbidding the employment of Indians in capturing deserters; for during the proceeding summer five
soldiers started early in the morning across the strait to
the American main, and made by the Indian path for

Michilimackinac . . . The commandant sent half-a-
dozen Indians after them, who in a couple of days
returned with the men's heads in a bag.

Although aware of the border question and its uncertain-
ty, the beleaguered British garrison was shocked when the
1828 International Boundary Commission awarded
Drummond Island to the United States. Once again the
British were uprooted. The mood was bittersweet that snowy
November as the brig *Duke of Wellington* and the schooner
Alice Hackett shipped the remaining ninety-one soldiers and
their families to their new post at Penetanguishene on
Georgian Bay. The two vessels were packed so tight with military supplies that personnel were permitted to take only a
few personal effects. As a result, many of the chairs, sofas,
dressers, and beds ended up at Fort Michilimackinac while
the nearby Indian village confiscated livestock and two thousand bushels of potatoes—paltry compensation for raising
the many children the soldiers and traders had sired and
deserted. *Today, the fort site is gone, replaced by an operating quarry.*

The Commandant's house at Fort Drummond, 1820

DeTour

Misadventures of a Stolen Mill

As the sun broke over the horizon on that chilly morning in April 1889, Bill Jones' old nag laboured on with ragged breath. Would the poor creature last the fourteen-hour journey to Pickford so Jones could telephone the sheriff in the Sault? What was the urgency? A robbery. The DeTour sawmill had been stolen! In a brilliant heist, abetted by their lawyer, the Moiles brothers, Jim, George, Henry and Charles, had used the cover of darkness to steal one of the town's main employers. Although the town was mostly unaware, the mill had been declared insolvent, and the company's Chicago creditors had posted guards to prevent the owners from removing any machinery. The brothers came up with an ingenious scheme to get around the guards.

They chose a busy election day for the arrival at DeTour of their nephew, Johnny Moiles' with his steam tug, the *Tom Dowling*, and two scows. In retrospect, the clues were obvious. Traditionally, the first vessel entering the harbour after spring break-up sounded its horn to inaugurate a new shipping season. But the *Tom Dowling* slipped quiet and unnoticed up to the dock. About fifty men jumped out and hurried into the mill. "Time for an overhaul—get her ready for the season," explained one of the Moiles' to the guard and a few bystanders. The wholesome-looking boys exhibited such exuberant confidence that no one questioned them. They offered the guard some whiskey and, after a short time, played their ace. Knowing that the guard's wife was pregnant, no sooner did the conspirators announce that she was in labour, than the anxious, unsuspecting watchman raced off.

With no time to waste, the crew stealthily loaded the stripped mill onto the tug. Everything was taken, even the nails holding the siding. The value of what remained, minus the real estate, was a paltry $5.00. Before pulling away from DeTour, they cut the village's telephone line. By the time the sheriff in Pickford was notified, the mill would be in Canadian territory heading for its new home on John Island. It must have seemed the perfect crime. But someone had forgotten to tell the brothers that it was April 1, 1889—April Fool's Day.

Hours later, the sheriff and his deputies followed the trail of open water through the ice and right to the boats which had become stuck fast in the ice. As the posse approached, one of the Moiles brothers appeared on deck brandishing a rifle. According to John Nevill's book, *Wanderings*, Moiles shouted, "the boat and her tow is in Canadian waters and you can't touch her. The first men among you who tries to set foot on any of these vessels gets a bullet through the head!" The pursuers prudently retreated. Besides, they were rather uncertain where the international border lay.

Because of the ice, the fugitives had little choice but to wait for nightfall, and then skulk back toward DeTour without their running lights. They tried a new route, grinding through the ice of False DeTour Passage, but they were again stopped dead between Drummond and Cockburn Islands. The mood turned sour. No one had bargained on being stuck in a half-frozen channel. If there had been an alternative escape route, the Moiles' would surely have suffered a full-scale mutiny. At long last, they spotted another tug, the *Pathfinder*. Seeing the crew of the *Tom Dowling* so tired and anxious, the captain was more than happy to come to their assistance. Working as a team, the boats eventually broke through to John Island. The *Pathfinder* departed, unwitting accomplice to a crime. One of the most unusual mill communities on the North Channel would ultimately spring up around the rebuilt mill (see John Island Mill, p.112).

DeTour Village

The native peoples called the site "point we go aground in our canoes" but traders and voyageurs renamed the point *La De Tour*, "the turn." It was here, at the traditional Indian stopping place, that their trading canoes laden with tools, trinkets, guns and whiskey turned west towards the most important fur trading post on the Upper Great Lakes: Fort Michilimackinac situated at the juncture of Lake Huron and Lake Michigan.

DeTour's former coaling facility, one of the largest on the river

After the American Revolution, the 1783 Treaty of Paris drew the Canadian-American border from the Atlantic Ocean through the Great Lakes to Lake of the Woods. Disappointed British fur traders were loath to abandon regions in which they had forged strong alliances, but tensions grew as American fur traders began to challenge their right to be on U. S. soil. At DeTour in 1808, U.S. Indian Agent John Campbell and Lewis Crawford, a British trader, fell into a drunken argument. Purportedly started over a bottle of whiskey, it ended in a duel. Campbell, the American, was mortally wounded, and was taken to the nearest medical practitioner, at the British fort on St. Joseph, where he died.

Early inhabitants of DeTour relied on fishing and lumbering. As more and more traffic was attracted to the St. Mary's waterway, DeTour became an important wood-fuelling depot, and later, one of the largest coal suppliers in the area. As for off-hour diversions, according to early jail records, these had some connection to charges of "drunk and disorderly" behaviour! Those of Scottish and English descent usually got off with paying only court costs. But for any Indians, Mexicans, French or Irish, a stiff fine of $1.00, or a ten-day jail sentence was also meted out.

The original spelling of the town's name remained the same for 200 years until the community gained highway access. Faced with signs reading, "Detour 32 miles," motorists were totally confused until the name was changed to DeTour. Discover the town's history by visiting the DeTour Passage Museum. The region's past comes alive through fascinating photographs and displays of antiques, marine artifacts and a rare Fresnel lens rescued from DeTour Reef lighthouse.

The Tragic End of Drummond Island's First Ferry

For those eking out a living along the St. Mary's, a boat was a necessity. Nothing like the majestic schooners and paddlewheelers that sailed by in the shipping lanes, these boats did provide transportation and often another source of income by shuttling people, food, livestock and mail between communities. At the end of the nineteenth century, Daniel Murray Seaman Jr. won the U.S. postal contract for Drummond Island. His 36-foot motor launch, *Clyde*, made regular trips to DeTour, Raber, Lime Island and other smaller hamlets.

Life was lost when the Clyde *foundered*

One October night in 1908, Murray and Sarah Jane Seaman, their 17-year-old son Clyde, and a friend were headed to the Sault for gasoline and supplies. Suddenly, a ship loomed out of the darkness at them. The *John P. Donaldson* rammed them with a monumental jolt, and their tug started to sink. Murray and his wife Sarah Jane grabbed whatever they could to stay afloat. But where was their son Clyde? When the collision occurred he had been tinkering in the engine room. Sadly, it was not until the following spring that Clyde's body was recovered by the lighthouse tender *Aspen*.

The *Clyde* was replaced by the *Naida*, which plied the same route until 1915 when Seaman limited her service to the run between DeTour and Drummond Island. After Henry Ford introduced his Model T, Seaman realized that those lucky enough to own a car would want to drive to Sault Ste. Marie so the *Naida* began taking one car each run. By 1922, roads had improved and the increase in the number of cars encouraged a competitor to launch a bigger ferry, the *Drummond*.

Today ferries still ply the waters between DeTour and Drummond Island. While waiting to depart, visitors can drop into the DeTour Passage Museum conveniently located at the ferry terminal.

FORT ST. JOSEPH

The Military Siberia of Upper Canada

1794. The British garrison was displeased at having to relocate to a small arm of land on the south-east tip of St. Joseph Island. After the American Revolution (1776-83), their former Fort Michilimackinac on Lake Michigan was awarded to the United States. The British managed to defy the order to vacate for twelve years but finally, with the signing of Jay's Treaty in 1794, they were forced to move to St. Joseph Island. As strategic locations go, it was far less desirable than Mackinac Island, which lay in the narrows between Lakes Huron and Michigan—essential for control of the western fur trade. Still, the location of the St. Joseph Fort had some strategic and economic merit: it was on the direct route for canoes heading back to Montreal with furs, and for ships navigating the St. Mary's River.

Fort St. Joseph, nicknamed "the military Siberia of Upper Canada"

By 1796, the military site on St. Joseph Island was cleared and timbers were squared for new buildings. Soldiers and artisans began to grumble about the official policy which provided free accommodation for higher ranking personnel but absolutely no support for the others. The disgruntled spokesmen—a blacksmith, a storekeeper and an interpreter—confronted Lieutenant Johnson to know why they should be forced to build within the military compound at their own expense. Judging from their unhappy experience at Michilimackinac (where they were forced to abandon all they had built) they well knew how badly the whim of military politics could affect their businesses. After much discussion, they were permitted to construct their businesses outside the walls and they were soon joined by fur traders and merchants allied with Britain. In addition to being a military post, the island was headquarters for the Indian Department which supervised the annual gift-giving ceremony.

Heading up the construction was a fresh-faced eighteen year old, Lieutenant George Landmann of the Royal Engineers. Only his second season in Canada, he adapted surprisingly well to the unfamiliar frontier conditions:

> My hut was about twenty feet square, formed of logs in the usual way, but had no chimney; this defect was remedied by a wide space paved in the middle for the fire-place, and a hole two feet square in the roof to let out the smoke—for there was no ceiling and no boarded floor, but it could boast of one window with oiled paper, a tolerably good substitute for glass.

His weekly food rations consisted of "three pints of dried peas, six ounces of butter, six ounces of rice, four pounds of salt pork—the pork and butter rancid from being salted fifteen to twenty years ago."

Just back from a trip to Quebec, Landmann was immediately requested to journey to Sault Ste. Marie to obtain money to pay the labourers, a seemingly straightforward task. It was, however, to take on nightmarish qualities. Accompanied by two traders, he arrived at the Sault and discovered there was no money available. He would have to continue on to Mackinac Island. Once in possession of the silver, the Lieutenant was anxious to leave Mackinac as quickly as possible. His Indian guides, however, insisted on first making offerings and prayers to the manitous who controlled the wind and the weather. After each lengthy speech, the Indians with carefully averted eyes, would toss some tobacco into the lake. It was only after the offerings were finished that they set off.

Within hours, it became apparent their prayers were not being answered. Their canoe was on the verge of capsizing in a gale-force storm. Lt. Landmann did not know what terrified him more, the prospect of drowning or the prospect of telling his commander that $2,000 in silver lay on the bottom of the lake. Tying a braid of leather to the money chest, he tossed it overboard to serve as an anchor. For twenty-four long hours, they battled the raging waters before reaching the comparative safety of Little Mackinac Island.

For days, they were lashed by driving rain. What little food they had was long gone. To Landmann, even twenty-year-old rancid pork would have tasted like ambrosia. By the eleventh day he understood the meaning of starvation. The Indians, more acquainted with empty stomachs, set some water on a fire and one by one dropped their shoes in to boil. Hours later they drank the water and chewed the leather. Landmann eventually returned to the fort, shoeless and thinner, but carrying the silver.

At the western entrance to Lake Huron, Fort St. Joseph, was dubbed "the military Siberia of Upper Canada." Furthest west in a serpentine string of British North American forts that began on the St. Lawrence River, its distant location meant it was often short-changed on provisions. One winter the supply of winter jackets failed to arrive and so some Hudson's Bay blankets were converted into coats. They proved so functional that these coats became both a military and civilian tradition.

The extreme isolation of Fort St. Joseph often bred discontent and encouraged desertion. In 1809, a search party was dispatched to find two deserters. By the time they were found, one man was dead and the other so badly frostbitten that his legs and fingers had to be amputated. At these forts, surgical procedures were often quite primitive. The St. Joseph medic was a Scotsman named Brown. Although he had a reputation for being cruel, he was compassionate compared to the surgeon at Michilimackinac. Dr. William Beaumont had decided to conduct experiments on a patient suffering from a large bullet wound in the abdomen. The doctor had him swallow various foods and meats tied to a string and observed the length of time it took to digest them.

When Captain Charles Roberts assumed command of the struggling British Fort, the United States had become unwillingly embroiled in European politics. During the French Revolution (1789-99) and the Napoleonic Wars between France and Great Britain (1799-1815), both countries continually violated the maritime rights of the neutral United States. American ships were stopped on the high seas by British naval vessels looking for British deserters and British citizens. In this way thousands of American seamen, especially naturalized Americans of British origin, were impressed into the Royal Navy. In addition, both France and Britain issued Orders-in-Council which allowed them to seize any American vessels that sailed directly to the other's ports. Between 1803 and 1812, nearly 1,500 American ships were charged with trading with the enemy. Because these measures threatened their neutrality and played havoc with their export trade, the United States Congress declared war on June 18, 1812. Suddenly, Fort St. Joseph, the forgotten garrison at the end of the line, became the key to securing the Upper Great Lakes.

War of 1812: The British Attack
Fort Michilimackinac

July 12, 1812. Captain Charles Roberts eyed the hodge-podge army wearily: his forty soldiers (older men fit only for garrison duty); over 400 Indians who were restless for action; and 160 voyageurs. After a fine military service in India and Ceylon, how did he end up here? Fort St. Joseph was hardly the crown jewel. It wasn't even fortified: the partially-completed log palisade had never been adequately repaired after collapsing in a wind storm. His only chance for victory was to act offensively and strike the Americans while he could still count on the element of surprise. But his hands were tied. Roberts had known of America's declaration of war since July 3, yet now he had to wait to be given official authority to attack Fort Michilimackinac from General Isaac Brock, who was in charge of all British forces in Upper Canada.

Roberts spied an advancing canoe and paced as the winded voyageur landed. The Captain scanned the note and passed it to fur trader Robert Dickson (called *Mascotapah* by the natives, meaning "Redhead man").

FORTS OF THE ST. MARY'S RIVER

CANADA

Fort Brady
Built 1822

ST. JOSEPH IS.

USA

Fort St. Joseph
built 1796, burned 1814

DRUMMOND IS.

British Landing

Fort Drummond
built 1815

Fort Michilimackinac
(Mackinac Island)
built 1782

LAKE
MICHIGAN

LAKE HURON

Fort Michilimackinac
built 1715

The Scotsman spat out the message with disbelief, "Brock wants us to hold off on hostilities!" Roberts knew why Dickson was anxious—the 123 natives he had brought for this offensive would soon head home if they did not see action shortly.

Three days later, a messenger arrived with ambiguous orders from Brock. Roberts chose to interpret them as approval for an attack of Fort Michilimackinac. Led by the fife and drum, the troops marched to the wharf and boarded the North West Company sailing vessel, the *Caledonia*, which Roberts had commandeered. The small armada was an impressive sight—the *Caledonia* with its two cannons surrounded by British regulars in scarlet red coats; traders from the Sault; ten bateaux each filled with 160 voyageurs in their colourful sashes; and seventy canoes carrying hundreds of Indians adorned in war paint and feathers led by such notable chiefs as Grizzly Bear, Black Wolf, The Teal, and One-eyed Decorah.

They landed in the middle of the night on the northwest side of Mackinac Island at a spot now known as British Landing. The Americans, ignorant of the outbreak of war, were completely taken by surprise and surrendered without a fight (see Mackinac Island).

With the British garrison installed on Mackinac Island, Fort St. Joseph was completely vulnerable. Not surprisingly, in 1814 American soldiers retaliated by burning all the garrison buildings except for residences.

Today a museum at the excavated Fort St. Joseph displays military artifacts, uniforms and weapons from the 1800s. From the bridge leading to St. Joseph Island, Parks Canada "beaver" signs guide the visitor along a 51-km scenic drive to Fort St. Joseph National Historic Site.

MACKINAC ISLAND, LAKE MICHIGAN

Fort Michilimackinac: British Attack in 1812

July 16, 1812. His men could not paddle fast enough to escape the advancing flotilla of armed sailing ship, canoes and bateaux. Hauled on board the brig *Caledonia*, shocked American fur trader Michael Dousman stood before British soldiers and learned he was a prisoner of war. Dousman was on a reconnaissance mission to Fort St. Joseph. The commander at Fort Michilimackinac, Lieutenant Porter Hanks, became suspicious when he saw droves of Indians passing by his fort. Hanks knew tensions between America and Great Britain were at an all-time high, but he had received no official communications. When one of the Indians spoke of an impending attack, Hanks sent Dousman to quietly ferret out information from his fur trading friends at Fort St. Joseph.

The British were amused to hear Dousman knew nothing of the war. Today was July 16. On June 18, U.S. President James Madison had declared war on Great Britain and yet no messenger had informed the American fort. Michilimackinac was obviously ripe for the picking.

Dousman was surprised when the British Commandant, Captain Roberts, and Robert Dickson, an imposing six-foot Scotsman, offered him a proposition: Dousman would be allowed to evacuate the community lying outside Fort Michilimackinac if he would give his word not to alert Lieutenant Hanks or the garrison.

In the early hours of July 17, 1812, the British troops landed on the island. Under cover of darkness, Dousman and a man named Oliver alerted the community and herded them to a safe area. Meanwhile the Indian recruits congregated on the high ground, and a number of voyageurs hauled the cannon up the escarpment overlooking the garrison. Lieutenant Hanks awoke at dawn. Unnerved by an unusual silence surrounding the fort, he soon realized the cause. He jolted the sleepy American garrison into action. How could Michilimackinac's 57 soldiers hope to battle a force of 700 supported by a threatening cannon on the heights? Hanks surrendered without bloodshed and, by noon, the Union Jack was flying over the island.

Settlement evacuated under the cover of night before British attack on Fort Michilimackinac

Robert Dickson was relieved. He had feared the Sioux, Winnebago and Menominee under his command might have proven uncontrollable if a battle had broken out. However, the Indians would have to be mollified somehow. This was accomplished by distributing American trading goods and profits from the captured furs among the combatants.

Capturing Michilimackinac was almost like a homecoming. It had been built by the British in 1782, then lost when Lake Michigan became part of the United States after the American War of Independence. From a strategic point of view, the fort's capture was vital. With Fort Michilimackinac and Fort Detroit on Lake St. Clair under their flag, the British would control the Upper Great Lakes, Michigan territory, the Upper Mississippi and by extension, most of the western fur trade. Consequently, Britain had little difficulty recruiting the voyageurs to her side.

The Treaty of Ghent, signed Christmas Eve 1814, restored the pre-war international boundaries. And so, in 1815, U.S. troops returned to Michilimackinac. The disappointed British withdrew for a second time, this time to Drummond Island. Michilimackinac was renamed Fort Holmes in honour of Major Andrew Hunter Holmes, killed in a failed attempt to recapture the fort in August of 1814. Today it is known as Fort Mackinac while the name Fort Michilimackinac designates an earlier British fort on the mainland. Fort Mackinac is a popular tourist destination. Guided walking tours and reinactments of military drills delight the visitor. (See Drummond Island p.205 for the continuing saga of the peripatetic British garrison).

LIME ISLAND

Human History Thousands of Years Old

Vastly different water levels are recorded on Lime Island's shores, making it one of the most compelling archaeological sites in Michigan. Flint fragments left by tool-carving peoples six thousand years ago have been found on the highest reaches of the island. At one time, Lime and Cockburn Islands were connected by a flat stretch of land on which the Ojibwe are said to have played lacrosse. Their name for the larger island was *Pah-gah-dah-wah-min-is*, "Ball-Playing Island." In addition, natives buried their dead on the Island and took advantage of its bountiful hunting grounds.

The Island first appears on a 1744 French map as *Isle de Plastre* , "Island of Plaster." Did the French occupy the island and produce lime from kilns as the name suggests, or were they merely acknowledging the resource? In support of the former idea, it is worthwhile to note that while the French were precise in naming Isle de Plastre, they failed to name larger and more significant islands in the St. Mary's River. Sixteen lime kilns have been uncovered on the Island, some dating back an estimated 200 years. Claims that these kilns were used in the construction of the St. Joseph and Drummond Island forts have been discredited. Both forts had their own kilns.

In 1885 after farming the island for many years, Joseph Kemp sold the site to the Lime Island Manufacturing Company. Sold in barrels manufactured on the island, the lime was used for cement, mortar and plaster as well as tanning leather, making glass and neutralising alkaline soils.

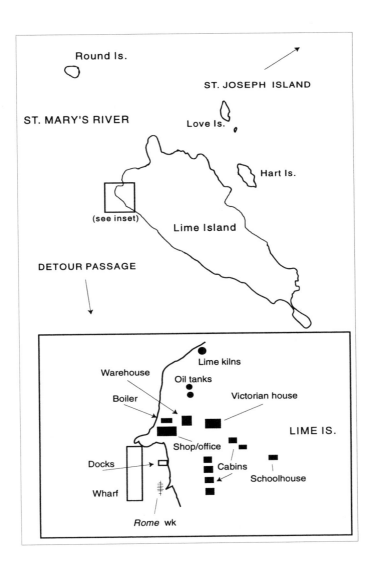

Round Is.

ST. JOSEPH ISLAND

ST. MARY'S RIVER

Love Is.

Hart Is.

(see inset)

Lime Island

DETOUR PASSAGE

Lime kilns

Warehouse

Oil tanks

Boiler

Victorian house

Shop/office

LIME IS.

Docks

Cabins

Schoolhouse

Wharf

Rome wk

1890s: The Grand Hotel Era

Five years after the Lime Island Manufacturing Company began production, the island took on a new persona. Lieutenant Francis Davenport from Detroit purchased the island as the site of a luxurious 30-room hotel. A graduate of the U.S. Naval Academy, Davenport served during the Civil War and later sailed the Great Lakes until his retirement in 1870. There was some speculation that the hotel was built to compete with the popular Grand Hotel on Mackinac Island, but most people felt the flamboyant Davenport merely wanted a private resort where he could entertain his wide circle of acquaintances. And entertain he did. Famous Hollywood stars such as Hoot Gibson, Mae West, and Lillian Russell basked in Lime Island's tranquil setting.

Although Davenport had many friends, they did not fill a hotel. So he established the St. Mary's Club. For a $25 initiation fee, $25 annual dues, and a rate of $1.00 per day or 50 cents for children under ten, members enjoyed billiards, fishing, sailing, swimming and pony rides for the young. Guests could even procure lime at 7 cents a barrel from the kilns, still operational until the early 1900s. Cows, chickens, turkeys and ducks were raised on the island, and according to the club's effusive brochure, fish was served at every meal with one or two meat dishes and "well cooked" vegetables.

The Community of the Coaling Depot

Davenport sold his island paradise to the Pittsburgh Steamship Company in the early 1900s and it was soon transformed. On a massive 900-ft. dock, steam-operated cranes filled hundreds of tons of coal into giant hoppers. Coal chutes spewed 100 to 250 tons of fuel into a vessel in less that twenty minutes.

The grand hotel was converted into four apartments for senior officials, and houses were built for the other employees (complete with gardens, chicken coops and corrals for livestock). The only thing missing was an impressive house for the superintendent. It was known that the Pittsburgh Steamship Company had a Victorian house on their abandoned coal-fuelling site on Point aux Frenes (see p.234). The problem was how to transport it to Lime Island.

Lime Island settlement in winter. The former hotel (right) with residences behind, school (top centre), Victorian house (left)

Smaller houses had been placed on skids and moved during the winter from Point aux Frenes to various locations. But moving a three-storey house to Lime Island was another matter. Muttering a few prayers, the men hooked teams of horses to the skids with logging chains and started off. The magnificent building was gliding across the frozen St. Mary's when suddenly the crisp air filled with a sickening creaking and moaning. As teamsters urged the horses to move faster, accompanying men hammered frantically on the back of the skids.

When they reached deeper water the men noticed that the tremendous weight of the house was creating a massive depression as they travelled along the ice. It was the longest two-and-a-half miles they had ever travelled. Reaching the safety of Lime Island, the men unanimously agreed that the best remedy for their distraught state was a visit to MacDonald's Saloon in Raber. Only later was the house rolled up the hill.

In order to create a more contented atmosphere at the isolated spot, the company favoured hiring men with families. For the women of the community, Lime Island offered particular challenges. The coal dock operated twenty-four hours a day, seven days a week, covering everything and everyone with a fine layer of soot. One mother exclaimed, "I washed three kids before I found one that was mine!"

Most of the families wintered on Lime. To get supplies from the mainland, some used a horse and sled, but most walked across the three miles of ice carrying boards to get over weak spots. During the summer, they depended on the company boat that left for Raber every day at eight a.m. and returned in late afternoon. Not every visitor was welcome. When the dogcatcher arrived and demanded $12 to licence all the island's dogs, the superintendent reluctantly handed over the money. Then the dogcatcher asked how he might get home. "We can take you," the superintendent grinned, "but it'll cost twelve bucks."

In the autumn of 1918, Michigan State was stricken by

a virulent flu epidemic. Sailors were so ill they climbed down from the ships and collapsed on the dock. After the ships departed, the dock was scoured with disinfectant in an effort to protect the community but to no avail. One resident was stricken and soon the entire community was bed-ridden. Only four healthy men remained to work the coal operation and to keep everyone's house fires stoked.

Lime Island coal dock, a messy business

In 1948 Northwestern Hanna Fuel Company bought the island and modernized the facility with steel loading towers fed by a conveyer belt. The company also installed two large insulated tanks for heated bunker crude. They sold 125 million gallons of fuel annually. Lime Island became the fastest fuelling operation on the Great Lakes, capable of pumping 1,600 gallons per minute into the more than 800 vessels that called in each season. When diesel-powered ships journeying from Duluth to Chicago without refuelling were introduced on the lakes, the facility began to lose its dominant position. In 1982, it closed.

Today Lime Island is considered to have one of the earliest and best-preserved industrial complexes on the upper Great Lakes. And thanks to over 6,000 hours logged by Department of Natural Resources personnel and volunteers, the island's unique history has been preserved and her natural beauty restored. The Victorian house, the schoolhouse and a few cabins have been rebuilt. The lime kiln site, a quarter of a mile north of the dock, can be observed from a wooden walkway which serves to protect the kilns from possible damage and visitors from poison ivy. Along the island's several miles of cleared trails, rare flowers, animals and birds (including nesting Blue Herons in season) can be observed. Tent platforms are available on a first come, first served basis.

A narrow-gauge railroad brought timber to the Raber Sawmill

Raber

With a rattling release of the schooner's anchor chain, William Raber and Captain Feltes arrived at the site of the future town of Raber where Scotsman John Stevenson had lived a solitary existence since 1878. The two men did not set themselves up as aspiring founding fathers. Rather they were seeking their fortunes in the lumber trade. But thanks to a seemingly inexhaustible supply of logs, a community of three hundred soon sprang up and the high-pitched sounds of milling machinery filled the air. Offshore, a fleet of schooners lay waiting to load cedar ties, posts and board lumber.

To simplify and speed up the movement of logs, the Mud Lake Lumber Company laid down three narrow gauge tracks, extending out like spokes from the mill into the forest. When wood was depleted in one area, the track was simply pulled up and moved to another. The only drawback was the number of fires in the dry season started by showering sparks from "Old Mag," the locomotive's wood-fired engines.

At the turn of the century, Raber's wooden plank sidewalks were lined with homes, saloons, stores, a barbershop, company boarding house and dance hall. Although life in Raber was somewhat insular, a strong, active community kept it from being dull. Musical groups blossomed and Fourth of July celebrations were a highlight with baseball, greased pig contests, log burling and log rolling. Weddings were a communal affair with everyone contributing to a giant potluck dinner. Even the backwoods lumbermen would show up to drop a month's wages in the hat in order to dance with the bride or one of her bridesmaids. Hotels and boarding houses were often so busy that local residents were encouraged to take in boarders. Outside town, most roads were muddy, rock-strewn oxen trails and so most shipping and public transportation was by done by water. A round trip to the Sault cost $2.50.

ROUND ISLAND LIGHTHOUSE

Erected in 1892, the classic white lighthouse on Round Island lords over the St. Mary's River. The lanternroom glass had a red sector. Sailors approaching the light upbound were in good water if they saw only white light emanating from the lighthouse, and in danger of shoals if they could see some red.

POINT AUX FRENES

A Shocking Surprise

A new era dawned near the turn of the century, when the numerous wood-fuelling docks were replaced by a few coaling depots. Point aux Frenes was purchased by the Pittsburgh Steamship Company in 1907 and renamed Pittsburgh Landing. Soon, large lake freighters en route to and from Lake Superior were frequenting its dock. Houses were built for the management, along with a three-storey rooming house and a blacksmith shop. Pittsburgh Landing was destined to be a huge success.

Late one evening, the crew exchanged nervous glances. Was it an earthquake? Everyone froze waiting for the tremor to stop, but it didn't. Instead, the shaking dock groaned and shifted dangerously. Pilings snapped like toothpicks. As frantic men jumped into the frigid black water, the dock disappeared, driven under by the weight of coal and machinery. This was impossible! Before building, the company had checked the riverbed thoroughly—it was hard as rock. It was hard, yes, but not because it was bedrock. The bottom was made of "water clay," a substance which is extremely hard unless disturbed. The continual loading and unloading of coal caused the dock pilings to shake and the constant movement turned the clay to mush.

The Pittsburgh Steamship Company salvaged what it could and rebuilt their coal fuelling centre on Lime Island in 1910.

MUNUSCONG LAKE

The Most Expensive Raft on the St. Mary's

As recounted in Bruce Martin's *The Island of St. Joseph and St. Mary's River*, it was the lure of wealth that motivated the Richardson brothers—Abbot, William, Fred, and Richard—to fell trees from dawn until dusk in the mid-1800s. On their dock at Munuscong Lake, stacks of cord wood mounted higher and higher and their dreams of riches and hopes for the future grew with them. Soon the navigation season would open and the Richardsons, like the Rains' brothers at Sailors Encampment, would make a fortune selling fuel to hungry ships. Unknown to them, the St. Mary's had other plans . . .

As the warm spring winds began to gust down the lake, the honeycomb ice broke free. Driven by a powerful wind, masses of drifting ice slammed against the dock. The pilings groaned under this terrific pressure. Then with a deafening crack, the whole dock tilted into the frigid water. Open-mouthed, the four men watched their dreams dissolve into the rushing water.

ST. JOSEPH ISLAND: SAILORS ENCAMPMENT

All Things Troublesome With the St. Mary's River

Bored, two sailors stared dully at the fishing lines dangling through holes in the ice and pondered their career choice. Behind them sat their snow-covered schooner, locked in the frozen St. Mary's River.

Sailors Encampment was named to honour the men trapped on St. Joseph's Island over a long winter in the 1830s. In time, it would become synonymous with the general frustration felt by all who had to navigate this menacing stretch of the St. Mary's River.

Sailors Encampment was the traditional stopping place for schooners heading up Lake George to Sault Ste Marie. Because Hay Lake (Lake Nicolet) was shallow and blocked by two sets of rapids, Lake George was the only feasible route. At night, sailors would congregate on shore, swapping stories, drinking grog, singing sea shanties, awaiting daylight and favourable winds. They were not about to challenge the St. Mary's River with its lethal shoals, swift current and torturous turns, except under the most promising conditions.

By 1852, schooners were giving way to smoky steamers and Sailors Encampment became an important fuelling depot operated by Tudor Rains. Steamers needed three hundred cords of wood per trip. At $1.50 a cord, it was no wonder Rains was a happy man. To augment this lucrative business, he and his brothers offered their services as river pilots.

Sailors Encampment, named after a lone ship became frozen in the ice

Concerned about the safety of the waterway above Sailors Encampment as traffic increased, the shipping companies began to pressure the government for improvements to the riverbed. They petitioned for an increase in depth to accommodate deeper-draft vessels and for better navigational aids to permit travel by night. Between 1856 and 1906, engineers cut, dredged and dynamited the river's eastern and western stretches from the middle of Neebish Island to the top of Hay and George Lakes. The changes would prove to be a huge boon to shipping but would push Sailors Encampment into the shadows. By 1900, coal-burning ships had eliminated the need for wood-fuelling depots and Sailors Encampment became a forgotten destination. But late at night at this favoured spot, eerie echos whisper in the trees, and dance out over the waves.

WEST NEEBISH ROCKCUT

Ancient Treasures Revealed

Even though the 1894 opening of Hay Lake (Lake Nicolet) was a boon to ship traffic using the St. Mary's River, the navigational problems were not completely solved. The only entrance to both Hay and George Lakes was through the Munuscong Channel. If an accident occurred, travel became a nightmare. That is exactly what happened when in 1899, the *Douglass Houghton* sank, completely blocking the waterway. There is some dispute whether the Houghton sank after being slammed by a barge it was towing or whether the *Douglass Houghton* and the steamer *John Fritz* both sank after a collision. Either way, shipping was paralysed. While older ships with a twelve-foot draft could still pass, deeper-draft vessels were out of luck. In total, 350 ships were blocked for ten days. The need to open a sister channel, West Neebish, was

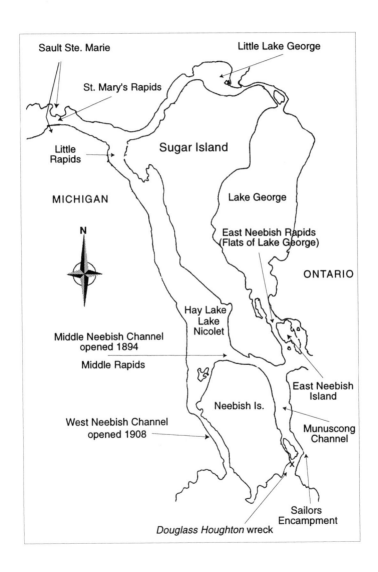

Sault Ste. Marie

Little Lake George

St. Mary's Rapids

Sugar Island

Little
Rapids

MICHIGAN

Lake George

N

East Neebish Rapids
(Flats of Lake George)

ONTARIO

Hay Lake
Lake
Nicolet

Middle Neebish Channel
opened 1894

Middle Rapids

East Neebish
Island

Neebish Is.

West Neebish Channel
opened 1908

Munuscong
Channel

Sailors
Encampment

Douglass Houghton wreck

now indisputable. With two channels, traffic could be completely separated: upbound boats on Lake George and downbound ones on Hay.

Work on the West Neebish Channel began in 1904. Two dams were constructed to hold back the force of the St. Mary's and after several days of pumping, the channel was almost empty except for a few freshwater clams. A limestone wall was clawed out, so smooth a ship could safely rub alongside. But how were they to create a flat floor? The contractor, Mr. Locker, came up with a solution. Lateral and longitudinal holes, two-inches deeper than the required floor depth, were drilled at intervals of fifty feet, then pipes were cemented into the holes and connected to water pipes. Under tremendous pressure, water was pumped into the limestone. As the hours passed, anticipation rose. Slowly, the floor began to lift. After it had risen four inches, the pumps were switched off. The result justified Locker's optimism. After the loosened rock was removed, he could see that the water had split through the weakest level of stratification leaving a surface as smooth as a kitchen floor.

A surprise awaited them. Millions of years ago, this had been the bottom of a tropical sea. Hundreds of fossils of early creatures including primeval squids called Nautiloids, some as monstrous as twelve feet long, with head and tentacles protruding from the wide end of a long cone-shaped shell, were embedded in the rocks. Astonishingly, nothing was done to preserve them. Except for those fossils in the channel floor, all the rock was carted away to be used for landfill.

In 1908, the $1 million channel was completed. Once called "boiling water" by the Indians, West Neebish had been transformed from a narrow stream of shallow, lively water into a 300-foot wide, 23-foot draft entrance into Hay Lake, gateway to Lake Superior and the West.

EAST NEEBISH

Snagged on the "Flats of Lake George"

Whistling merrily, the Rains Brothers pulled alongside the ship grounded in the East Neebish channel and offered their assistance. The brothers may have been scorned as vultures and parasites but when something went wrong they were a welcome sight. In 1875, Allen Rains and his brother Norman carried on a thriving business lightening ships that exceeded the channel's fourteen-foot draft. The problem? A limestone bar which created treacherous rapids through East Neebish and had been a sailor's nightmare for years, certainly as far back as 1822. In that year, Colonel Hugh Brady, Indian Agent Henry Rowe Schoolcraft and 250 soldiers were en route to the Sault to construct Fort Brady. Warned beforehand by the hired pilot that their chances of passing the rapids were slim, Brady took on board three 35-foot voyageur canoes. The pilot was correct and they were forced to drop anchor before East Neebish. While the troops proceeded to the fort site by canoe, the sailors were left to unload enough cargo to allow the steamer to pass over the bar.

As traffic increased, so did the limestone bar's notoriety. In order to avoid being snagged on the "flats of Lake George," crews took pride in estimating precisely the amount of allowable cargo. Of course, it was in their own interest to do so since a mistake would require the unloading and reloading of the ship. A letter written in 1836 to the Sault agent of the American Fur Company reveals this frustration: "I cannot but recommend never to overload a vessel bound for this place. 7 1/2 feet is all the water we have on the bar . . . If they have to carry part of the loading on shore, it is not easily accomplished in a gale wind . . . Add to that, the loss of a fair wind, which may possibly detain the vessel a week or more below."

The rapids and limestone bar continued to be the nemesis of large craft trying to pass into Lake George. Although the Canadians carried out some dredging operations, it was not until 1883 that the Americans returned and succeeded in giving the channel a more accommodating sixteen-foot draft.

LAKE GEORGE

Troubles with Washington

In 1857, Captain George Whipple, head of an American dredging operation on Lake George, wondered why his Indian workers were looking at him strangely. If only they had told him that the middle of the lake was deeper, he might not be in this predicament. How was he to phrase a letter to Washington explaining why $27,000 had been wasted in surveying the west side of Lake George instead? Captain Whipple knew that the previous year, President Franklin Pierce had vetoed a bill to spend $100,000 to deepen the channel but his veto had been boldly overridden by Congress. Any potential embarrassment would now be most unwelcome to his superiors. His assessment was accurate and he was denied permission to switch the operations to the middle of Lake George. Another $10,000 was spent before Whipple's conscience got the better of him. He wrote a second letter, this time directly to the Secretary of War, who set up a commission to investigate the project. Dredging resumed in June 1858, this time in the middle of the lake.

Once finished, the channel was 150 feet wide with a depth between 14-18 feet. To everyone's frustration, the depth slowly reverted to 12 feet due to silt washed down by the current.

Dredges work to make a passable channel around the foundered Peck *and* Adams *on Lake George.*

HAY LAKE (LAKE NICOLET)

As a result of the pressure of increasing ship traffic, it became obvious that Hay Lake had to be made accessible to boats drawing more than four feet. Alterations began at the two-mile-long Middle Neebish Rapids in 1882. At the height of the operations, twenty dredges were working non-stop, six days a week.

In 1891, some of these dredges were commandeered to create a temporary channel around two sunken ships. In a narrow section of the Lake George channel, the down-bound steamer, *Susan E. Peck*, had collided with the upbound *George W. Adams* being towed by the steamer *Aurora*. According to Bernard Arbic's *Sugar Island Sampler*, the operation took four days, by which time Mud Lake (Munuscong Lake) was clogged with 75 vessels. This accident convinced the authorities that up and down bound traffic must be divided between Hay Lake and Lake George. According to a 1891 news item, there had been eight collisions in the previous five-year period alone.

Within two years, Hay Lake was ready for traffic, equipped with the most modern range lights and navigational aids. It officially opened in 1894, with the passage of the *Northwest*, a palatial passenger steamer on its maiden voyage to Duluth. Lauchlen Morrison, one of the engineers who worked Hay Lake, was on board. He wrote,

> . . . the passengers congregated on the forward lower deck gazing at us in wonderment, and taking our photographs. The captain of the ship was

standing nervously by, aghast at the idea of sup-
posed landlubbers handling the ship in unknown
and untried waters. Little did he know how well we
knew what lay below the keel of the ship!

The ship's safe passage was heralded by all as a major
accomplishment. According to the locals, however, this
was really the second ship to pass through Hay Lake.
Three years earlier, Owen Rains of Sailors Encampment
had quietly piloted through the steam barge *O.O.
Carpenter*. His feat was not intended to attract media
attention but was perhaps, a last hurrah for all those
pilots no longer needed to guide ships through this section of the St. Mary's.

Cramped conditions in floating bunkhouses

SUGAR ISLAND

The International Boundary

Following the War of 1812, commissioners representing Great Britain and the United States were appointed to draw the international boundary through the Great Lakes. The first step was to carefully study the original boundary as defined in the 1873 Treaty of Paris. This document clearly described the international border as running through the centre of the Great Lakes, but one vital link was missing. Where was the boundary for the St. Mary's River? Other documents were examined without success. The decision now rested with the commissioners.

Negotiations went relatively well. Drummond Island was assigned to the United States (much to the chagrin of the British garrison stationed there) and the remainder of the Manitoulin chain of islands to Great Britain. St. Joseph Island became British while Neebish was handed to the Americans. However, when it came to sixteen-mile long Saint George's Island, as Sugar Island was then called, heated conflict erupted.

The U.S. put forth two compelling arguments. First, it had been agreed that land would be divided equally between the two countries. As Britain already had been assigned the large St. Joseph Island, possession of Sugar would make her holdings grossly disproportionate to those of the U. S. Secondly, each country was to have a navigable channel within its borders. A British flag on Sugar would force the Americans to use the eastern portion of the St. Mary's River, called Hay Lake (Lake Nicolet), which at the time was only navigable by canoes and small boats. In its rebuttal, Great Britain pointed out that the issue of ownership concerned only river locations that were not dealt with in the Treaty of Paris. Therefore, the only islands open to debate were Neebish and Sugar. And if the U.S. was determined to take Neebish, it was only fair that Sugar go to Britain. The two countries remained at loggerheads for decades until the Webster-Ashburton Treaty of 1842 awarded Sugar Island to the United States.

An Island Of Two Countries

Although under the flag of the United States, Sugar Island was inextricably connected to both countries. Formerly known as St. George's Island, it acquired its new name from the original Indian designation *Sisibakwato Miniss* or "Sugartree Island." In the 1840s, it was home to a mixed population of Indians, Scots, English, French Canadians and Americans. The economy was largely agricultural-based. In addition to crops and livestock, settlers produced cheese, butter, milk, maple syrup and wine. The local hay was of such fine quality that much of it was shipped down to the thoroughbred stables in Kentucky.

Church's Landing was one-stop shopping

One of the island's first entrepreneurs, Philetus Church, arrived with his family in 1845 and over time opened a small shipyard, wood-fuelling dock, trading post and lumber mill at Churchville Point, strategically situated on the shipping lanes. Church treated the Great Lakes area as one big Common Market. He sold everything—pickles, shingles, telegraph poles, maple sugar, fish—to communities along both shores. His store was ensured a steady supply of furs, blueberries, raspberries and baskets to sell, being so close to the Indian village of Garden River on the Canadian shore. At the peak of this operation, Church employed thirty-five Garden River residents. Today all that remains of Church's Landing is the fine two-storey family home (designed by his talented son Jesse), now listed in the National Register of Historic Places. (For more about the Church family see Harbor Island p.168). The island's close proximity to Canada sometimes provided a financial

Sugar Island family

advantage for the homesteaders. In the 1880s, Albert Larmie's grandson, Abe, would dogsled to Canada to sell wool where it fetched forty more cents a pound. Canada's reasonable prices were another attraction for American residents. In *Sugar Island Sampler*, Bernard Arbic relates the anecdote of "Mooney" Sebastian, who was returning to Sugar with a boatload of supplies. Mooney was intercepted by two U.S. customs officers who asked what he was bringing back. When he replied it was only flour and chicken feed, they admonished him: "Next time, at least cross at night!"

The World Hears of Sugar Island

In 1943, discussions began about a new international body to replace the failed League of Nations. Over a period of two months, delegates from fifty nations met to hammer out a charter for the United Nations (U.N.). Together they worked to outline goals of maintaining international peace and security and procedures for international cooperation in solving economic, social, cultural and humanitarian problems. In December 1945, the organization voted to establish its headquarters in the United States. An international committee was given the job of choosing a site from a list of twenty-two potential cities including Chicago, Miami, Philadelphia, New York, and two Canadian cities, Quebec City and Vancouver. Published in newspapers worldwide, the list puzzled some readers: it included a place in Michigan called Sugar Island!

The bid was the brainchild of former Michigan governor, the flamboyant, eighty-five-year-old Chase

Osborn. Osborn owned property on Sugar Island and was one of its biggest boosters. But it was in a much larger context that he promoted Sugar Island. Osborn saw the 5,500 mile unfortified Canada/U.S. border as a powerful symbol of the U.N.'s objective and so he began to promote Sugar Island as International Island. Osborn also pointed to the peaceful acquisition of Sugar Island by the Americans in the 1842 Webster-Ashburton Treaty as a perfect example of the U.N.'s pledge "to settle international disputes by peaceful means, to refrain from the threat or use of force." Despite Osborn's determined lobbying, a site on the East River in New York City was chosen to house the United Nations. Many on Sugar Island must have breathed a sigh of relief!

Chase Osborn put Sugar Island on the map when he submitted it as a possible site for the United Nations.

GARDEN RIVER FIRST NATION

Chief Shingwauk—"The White Pine"

Chief Shingwauk from the Crane Clan was revered for being a strong, eloquent, and forward-thinking leader. He and his warriors fought in the War of 1812 at Niagara, at Fort Michilimackinac and alongside the great Shawnee Chief, Tecumseh. But Shingwauk is most remembered on the North Shore and on Lake Superior as a powerful shaman, a member of the *Midewewin*, or Ojibwe healing society, and a wise counsellor to his people.

Over the years, the chief watched with sadness the effect of the fur trade on the Ojibwe. Instead of bringing prosperity, the fur trade had brought suffering, poverty and disease. Furthermore, a steady influx of settlers and thus a resulting pressure on Indian lands had come in the wake of the traders. Something had to be done. At the end of the Seven Years War, the Royal Proclamation of 1763 had formally recognized that Indian lands must be purchased by the British Crown before any settlement could take place. Land could not be acquired by the Crown except through voluntary surrender by the chiefs and people who had rights to those lands. As allies of Great Britain, the Ojibwe were promised that their nations and lands would be protected. Unhappily, attitudes began to change, and by the 1840s these promises were being pushed aside by new, overriding considerations. Rapid industrialization was creating a world-wide demand for copper and iron. Chiefs tried to stop the invasion of mining companies and prospectors onto their lands, but their protests fell on deaf ears; deafened, no doubt, by the

12,000 pounds sterling earned by granting mining licences on unsurrendered Indian lands. A speech given by Shingwauk in 1849 reveals his anger and despair:

> . . . Time wore on and you have become a great people, whilst we have melted away like snow beneath an April sun: our strength is wasted, our countless warriors dead, our forests laid low, and you have hunted us from every place as with a wand, you have swept away all our pleasant land, and like some giant foe you tell us, "willing or unwilling, you now must go from amid these rocks and wastes, I want them now. I want them to make rich my white children, whilst you may shrink away to holes and caves like starving dogs to die.

The stage was set for the Ojibwe to take a stand. They chose as their initial battleground a mine site at Mica Bay on Lake Superior. In November of 1849, Chief Shingwauk, along with Chief Nebinagojing from Batchawana and a group of warriors set out from the Sault armed with a small cannon picked up from sympathizers at the Hudson's Bay Post. Under cover of darkness, they arrived at Mica Bay undetected and fired the cannon into the night. The terrified miners were still pulling on their britches as they fled into the woods.

Troops were quickly dispatched from Montreal. After a slight delay due to ice near Sault Ste. Marie, the two chiefs were arrested, taken to Toronto and jailed for several weeks. Much to the government's annoyance, there was a legal hitch to prosecuting the Indians. Under the terms of the Royal Proclamation, the mining company had no legal right to be on the land in the first place. The situation had to be addressed and so in 1850, the very next year, vast territories were ceded to the Crown under the Robinson-Huron Treaty covering the North shore of Lake Huron (including the North Channel) and the Robinson-Superior Treaty covering the Canadian shore of Lake Superior.

For their reserve, Shingwauk's people chose their ancestral village at Kitigon Zeebee, meaning "Garden River." The river and surrounding verdant lands were rich with food, and the site had been continually occupied as far back as oral histories relate. Before Shingwauk died in 1854 he helped to establish a "teaching wigwam." His dream had always been for his people to learn various trades so that their futures would be secure. To emphasize the need for education, he walked all the way from Garden River to Toronto to petition for a school.

Although it was built, it developed through government intervention into a residential school with a mandate to

Chief Shingwauk and wife

assimilate native children, rather than into an autonomous native school. Today it is home to the main campus of Algoma University College. Garden River First Nation is petitioning to have the name changed to Shingwauk University College in honour of their Chief. St. John's Church, the town's oldest building, was erected over Shingwauk's grave.

ST. MARY'S RAPIDS

In The Beginning: Bawating

Legend holds that when an industrious beaver built a dam across the St. Mary's River, Lake Superior was created. Spotting the beaver, the giant trickster Nana'b'oozoo chased it up river. Although he started out a mile behind, the giant caught up in one bound. In his enthusiasm, he stomped on the dam, sending rocks and wood hurtling through the air, and creating the great falls and whirlpools of the St. Mary's Rapids.

Called *Bawating*, "water pitching over rock," St. Mary's Rapids is one of the most historic sites on the river. For centuries, thousands of Indians travelled here late each spring for the harvest of whitefish over the summer. It was a time to catch and smoke fish for the long, lean winter months ahead, and it was a time to celebrate the earth's renewal, to conduct business, and to rekindle old friendships. The Saulteur, the Ojibwe group that lived along the Rapids, were recognised as the guardians of the fishery and were highly respected for their expertise at running the rapids. While a sternman skillfully steered the canoe through the powerful rock-strewn waters, a bowman would scoop up fish with hoop nets. The Indians were not the only ones who relied on the succulent whitefish. Traders who came here to intercept fur-laden Indians savoured it as well. However, by 1905 the river had been radically altered by dredging and damming operations, and this ancient fishery was virtually destroyed.

Priests, Pageants and the Fur Trade

When Jesuit priests, Isaac Jogues and Charles Raymbault, arrived at Bawating in 1641, they renamed the river and rapids after their patron saint, Marie. Twenty-seven years later, a mission was built by Father Jacques Marquette who marvelled at how easily the Indians took to baptism. But while the Jesuit priests hoped to create a new Catholic society, France's "Sun King," Louis the XIV, saw the Indians as the key to solidifying France's commercial supremacy in America through the lucrative fur trade. He decided the time had come to take formal possession of the Upper Country (no doubt influenced by the 1670 formation

Saulteur Indians fished the rapids with hoop nets and canoes

of the English Hudson's Bay Company) and that the way to highlight this new relationship was to stage a pageant. Sault Ste. Marie was the perfect location.

In June 1671, teepees from bands representing fourteen nations spread along the shores inhabited by the Saulteur. The ceremony began with a procession of chanting, black-robed priests, followed by the king's representative, Sieur de Saint Lusson, walking with sword unsheathed, the sun glinting off his helmet. In honour of the occasion, the Indians had: "bodies greased and painted heads, heads crowned with feathers and horns, strings of bears' and moose's teeth about their necks, fur robes carelessly flung about their limbs." The procession snaked from the mission to a knoll (where the fountain stands today in Government Park) on which a giant cross and a cedar pole bearing the Royal Arms of France had been raised.

After a solemn blessing, Jesuit Father Claude Allouez turned toward the 2,000 faces and began a chilling account

France claims the region, Royal Proclamation, 1671

of the French King's power, "When he attacks, he is more terrible than the thunder: the earth trembles, the air and sea are set on fire by the discharge of his cannon; while he has been seen amid his squadrons, all covered with the blood of his foes, of whom he had slain so many with his sword that he does not count their scalps but the rivers of blood he sets flowing." Allouez went on to describe the extent of the French King's wealth: "He owns more towns in number than you have in people five hundred leagues around; his warehouses are filled with enough hatchets to cut down all your forests; kettles to cook all your moose . . ." After Allouez's impressive oration, St. Lusson took possession of the territory in the King's name, promising to protect all those tribes living within his domain.

In the days following the ceremony the natives returned to their villages. No written record exists of their impressions of the affair, but perhaps it is worth noting that as soon as the envoy departed, Saint Lusson's interpreter witnessed the Indians ripping the Royal Arms of France off the cedar pole.

The mission at the Sault was soon joined by a seigneury granted to Sieurs de Repentigny and de Miselle based on their promise to attract settlers. They also were granted a monopoly on the area's fur trade. A fort was erected in 1750 but the small settlement disappeared following the loss of Quebec to the British on the Plains of Abraham in 1759.

Instead of occupying the fort, the British who arrived in 1762 moved to Fort Michilimackinac (originally built by the French). At first, the Indians attacked English fur traders, loathe to believe that Great Britain's control was anything but temporary. Eventually they became staunch British allies, who played a vital role in the War of 1812.

TWO SAULTS: TWO COUNTRIES

EARLY SAULT STE. MARIE, MICHIGAN

John and Susan Johnston

In the late 1700s, fur traders began taking up residence near the old Indian village. Many of the French and Métis voyageurs and traders were married to native women. One of the more successful marriages was that of John and Susan Johnston (Oshauguscodaywayqua). Johnston, a greenhorn fur trader, immigrated from Belfast, Ireland in 1790. He had a rough start. On Lake Superior's Madeline Island he was robbed of his boat, fishing net and supplies by his five hired voyageurs. It was only thanks to the hospitality of Chief Wabojeeg of the La Pointe Band that he survived the winter. During the long cold months, Johnston and the chief's daughter fell in love. Her father, having witnessed too many failed unions between Indian women and transient traders, refused to sanction the marriage stating, "White man, I have noticed your behavior. It has been correct, but . . . your colour is deceitful. Of you, may I expect better things?" Wabojeeg told Johnston to return to Montreal. If he was still committed to his daughter after an absence Wabojeeg would bless the wedding. Which he did. Susan Johnston not only secured her husband's position among the Indians in the fur trade, but she also played a pivotal role in easing tensions between her people and the Americans (see Fort Brady).

John and Susan Johnston

Following Jay's Treaty in 1794, America began enforcing its borders in this region. British traders were forced to move across the St. Mary's to build their own community, resulting in over thirty abandoned buildings on the Michigan side. Before too many years, however, the Sault, Michigan was to see another incarnation . . .

Fort Brady

Playing along the river edge at Sault Ste. Marie, Indian children were the first to spot the squadrons of canoes filled with soldiers brandishing rifles, light glinting off their bayonets. As the children fled into the woods, adults warily greeted the visitors.

By nightfall, a military encampment had been set up about a hundred yards from the Indian village, consisting of about seventy voyageurs, Indians, soldiers, officials and scientists.

Michigan Governor Lewis Cass was not surprised by the cool reception he had received from the Ojibwe earlier in the day. They had little love for Americans. After all, this was 1820; it was not many years ago that Ojibwe had fought against the Americans in the War of 1812. But the Ojibwe were in Michigan territory now. In an attempt to sever British control of the Upper Lakes fur trade, Cass was determined to build a fort near the little hamlet at Sault Ste. Marie.

The next day Governor Cass wasted no time in explaining his purpose. He requested the Ojibwe to sign over lands for a fort, and furthermore, the fort would be built with or without their consent. His pronouncement was met with anger. A chief by the name of Sassaba, clothed in a scarlet British military uniform, violently stabbed his war lance into the ground and kicked over the gifts brought by the Americans. Turning on his heel, he marched away followed by the other warriors.

Governor Lewis Cass

The first Fort Brady

As the Governor contemplated his next move he noticed the Indians had raised the Union Jack over their community. Despising all things British, Cass stormed to the village and yanked down the flag. With his piercing eyes directed at Sassaba, he ground the cloth beneath his foot and snarled that the Americans would crush him and his nation in the same way.

As the American soldiers stood poised over their weapons, Susan Johnston arrived to mediate the situation. She counselled the chiefs that resistance was futile if not mad and went on to praise Cass as a man of character and honour. (He was staying in the Johnston home.) At the next meeting all the Ojibwe chiefs except Sassaba acknowledged, however reluctantly, the authority of the American Government. They signed a treaty ceding four square miles of land, reserving their right to fish the rapids in perpetuity.

Two years after Cass had laid the groundwork, 250

soldiers and their families under the command of Colonel Hugh Brady, arrived to construct Fort Brady. Despite their earlier reservations, the Ojibwe welcomed them by firing their rifles into the air. They were resigned to the American "invasion," as was nearby British trader, John Johnston, who provisioned the garrison with 1,200 bushel of potatoes and quantities of oats, peas and hay.

The thirty-three buildings that formed Fort Brady's compound stood for almost seventy years before being replaced in the 1890s. New Fort Brady, active until 1944, now belongs to Michigan State University.

THE "SOO" MICHIGAN

The influx of hundreds of soldiers and their families to this outback did much to bolster Sault Ste. Marie and attract other settlers to the area. In spite of the presence of the fort, the "Soo" retained a relaxed frontier town atmosphere. Travel writer Anna Jameson wrote in 1837, "The garrison may be very effective for ought I know, but I never beheld such an unmilitary looking set. When I was there today, the sentinels were lounging up and down in their flannel jackets and shirt sleeves, with muskets thrown over their shoulders—just for all the world like plowboys going to shoot sparrows." Her scrutiny of the community however failed to uncover one of Sault's most mysterious residents.

The year of Mrs. Jameson's visit, James Ord had come to the Sault as a sub Indian agent. Quaife and Bayliss' book *River of Destiny* sets out convincing evidence that

Ord was the son of George IV of England, born during his annulled marriage to Maria Fitzherbert. Brought up in the Ord family, James received periodic sums of what he termed "hush money." It is said he died disheartened because the truth of his royal lineage was never confirmed.

Perhaps Anna Jameson met another notorious resident, Reverend Abel Bingham, who railed at the excesses of the Sault: two billiard rooms, as many card tables as homes and liquor stocks of more than 15,000 gallons. He labelled the local Indians "a nation of drunkards" and accused the traders of providing enough liquor to keep an Indian drunk all day for the price of one whitefish.

Bingham began a religious revival and temperance movement at Fort Brady. And so, for a brief time, traders stopped importing grog. Yet this did not entirely stop the trafficking as liquor continued to arrive via the postal service or in shipments to local stores. The real shortage was in hay. According to Frederick Marryat, another travel writer to describe the early Sault, farmers had to travel up to thirty miles to find animal feed. This scarcity meant horses and cattle were regularly fed fish over the winter. One horse which became so fond of this odd diet, could be found hanging about the docks stealing fish.

The early "Soo" waterfront

As interest in Lake Superior's mineral wealth increased, so did the importance of the Sault as a provisions centre for prospectors, traders and settlers. There was one major stumbling block—how to haul cargo past the rapids. In 1839 Michigan State had made a feeble attempt to build a lock but the project was scuttled when disagreements broke out between the military and the contractor. In 1845, a unique system was devised using an over-land rail-way which ran around the falls on wooden metal-sheathed rails. Records from 1850 show the horse-drawn cars hauled about 6,000 tons of freight that season. It was inventive, but not efficient enough to answer the requirements for large-scale shipping on Lake Superior.

Shipping Adventures and the Rapids

Men cursed as they operated the steam winches, and oxen strained to drag the 261-ton steamer *Independence* along the cribbing and rollers. It took seven hellish weeks to portage the steamer up the Sault rapids in 1845. The rapids' half mile of white water and twenty-one foot drop presented a formidable barrier to opening Lake Superior to shipping. When the 118-foot *Independence* finally made it over the portage, however, it proved more than worth the effort; the steamer had a monopoly on serving the growing number of prospectors, traders, settlers and adventurers heading west.

On the evening of November 22, 1853 the *Independence* was at the "Soo," ready to sail with passengers, crew and 2,700 barrels of supplies and Indian trade goods. Suddenly, her boiler exploded, hurling people and debris down the rapids. Amazingly, though some were

Railway delivered freight to stores, 1850

severely injured, only four people perished.

At the moment of the explosion the Scottish purser, Jonas Watson, was carrying a satchel containing all the ship's money. He was shot like a human cannonball 150 feet through the air into the rushing torrent. His calls for help reached a woman who arrived in time to witness poor Watson clambering onto shore, the satchel still tightly in his grip—"a true Scotsman," everyone teased. Another casualty was sailor Amos Stiles who rode the wild rapids clinging to a bale of hay. Legend has it he never smiled again.

Pieces of the wreck were exhibited at the 1893 Chicago World's Fair but the full wreck was not salvaged until 1933 when the hulk was discovered during dredging operations. Captain Lauchlen Morrison wrote in a 1951 article for *Inland Seas*:

> There were round wooden match boxes filled with old sulphur matches, the smell of the sulphur still strongly evident. There were brass rings that had been gilt at one time, beads of all sizes and colours

as well as nine bottles of Indian trade whiskey.
Terrible stuff I know, for I sampled it.

The *Independence's* propeller is on display at the Upper
Park at the Michigan Sault locks.

Charles Harvey and the State Lock

In 1852, Vermont scale manufacturer E & T Fairbanks
Company sent a young salesman, Charles Harvey, to investigate Lake Superior's mineral potential. He returned with
an encouraging report of rich copper veins and proposed
that a canal and lock be built to provide access to the
region's wealth. In an effort to generate further interest,
Harvey appealed to Congress with a like-minded group of
financiers. Congress had already refused several requests
from the state of Michigan to build a lock. One politician
joked that building at the Sault would be as important as
putting a lock on the moon. Despite this kind of opposition, Congress passed a bill allowing right of way through
the Fort Brady military reservation and permitting
Michigan to donate 750,000 acres to the contractors to
finance the canal.

Harvey, the twenty-four-year-old neophyte, was promoted from scale salesman to General Agent in charge of
building the first ship canal in the United States and what
was the largest lock in the world at the time. A monumental task even for the most experienced, it was made more
daunting by the absence of labour, telegraph connections
and other supports necessary for a major construction project. To Harvey, the site might as well have been on the
moon!

On June 4, 1853, the steamer *Illinois* arrived bearing

Harvey, about a hundred labourers recruited from Detroit, and the necessary supplies. Looking for the workers, foremen travelled to New York City to recruit European immigrants as they disembarked at Ellis Island. Once assembled at the Sault, the 2,000 labourers had to contend with isolation, crowded living conditions and a devastating epidemic of cholera; Harvey struggled with other problems.

The remoteness of the site transformed minor difficulties into major dilemmas. Everything from mending to inventing tools required innovative solutions. The dredge proved useless when the reef near the entrance to the lock turned out to be rock and not sand, as indicated on the chart. Undaunted, the blacksmith shop came up with an ingenious iron punch. Attached to a thirty-foot oak shaft and operated by a portable steam engine, the punch generated several tons of striking force pulverising the rock twelve feet beneath the surface of the river. The punch is now on display at the River of History Museum in Sault, Michigan.

Charles Harvey

Harvey has been lauded by his biographers as "The Greatest Engineer," and "Young Mister Big," but in a 1965 article "Canalside Superintendent" published in *Inland Seas*, Ernest Rankin reveals the tension that developed between Harvey and Captain Augustus Canfield of the United States Topographical Engineers. Canfield warned that Harvey's shoddy building methods would compromise the lock. His concerns turned out to be well-founded as the State lock was repeatedly plagued with structural problems (see Drummond Island quarry p.166).

There was also criticism about the cost of the project. By May 1854, with the canal only half finished, J. W. Brooks was placed in charge. He was a backer and one of America's leading railroad builders. In less than a year, the *Illinois* locked through as the first steamer. It took eleven hours. Today it takes about twenty minutes.

Successive Locks:

Wietzel Lock: By 1870 more than a half million tons were passing through the State lock each year. Pressure was mounting to build a parallel lock. The $2.2 million, 515-ft.-long Wietzel lock was completed in 1881. The steamer *City of Cleveland* was the first vessel through in 1881. The lock had a 17-ft. draft, and an 80-ft. width in the chamber (60 ft. at the gates.)

Poe Lock: Before the Poe lock could be constructed, the State lock had to be destroyed. On completion in 1896, the new $3 million lock (704 ft. long, 100 ft. wide, 22 ft. draft) was the largest in the world, designed to accommodate four of the biggest ships in one locking.

Davis and Sabin Locks: Barely a decade later, the Davis and Sabin locks were under construction. The Davis was completed in 1914 while the Sabin's opening was delayed until 1919 because materials were difficult to obtain during the First World War. Each was 1,350 feet long. Together the two locks cost less than $4,700,000.

MacArthur Lock: In order to make room for the 800-ft. MacArthur Lock, the aging Wietzel lock had to be destroyed. It was completed in 1943. Lauchlen Morrison wrote of it in 1950, "It was built in 16 months, half the usual time. Everything was put underground and tunnels were run to all the operation machinery down some 70 feet in the rock below the locks. Down below, it was like a well-lighted city . . . This lock will take ocean-going tonnage of considerable draft."

The New Poe Lock: Construction of the new 1,200-foot-long Poe Lock began in 1961. Completed in 1968, its 110-foot width makes it the largest lock on the Great Lakes.

Constructing the Poe Lock, 1895

In addition to the Soo Locks Park and Historic Walkway, Sault Ste. Marie has many historic sites situated very conveniently one to another. The River of History Museum sits near or on the site of: the original Ojibwe (Chippewa) settlement, Marquette's 1668 mission, the site of St. Lusson's Pageant, the 1750 French fort, 1822 Fort Brady, and the Johnston, Schoolcraft, and Baraga Houses.

SAULT STE. MARIE, ONTARIO

1796: A Reluctant Move to the Canadian Sault

Grudgingly forced to leave the American Sault in 1796, the British subjects packed their possessions and sailed across the St. Mary's River to their new home on the Canadian shore. Most disheartened were the North West Company fur traders. Not only did the voyageurs have to portage around the rapids their thirty-five-foot canoes laden with tons of freight, (as they had on the American side) but now they also had to do it through mosquito-infested swampland. The remedy to the swampy problem was to build a small canal and lock. Completed in 1797, the system included a wharf, storehouses above and below the rapids and a lumber mill. Inside the lock, canoes and bateaux were raised nine feet then pulled by oxen along a 2,580-foot canal.

The "Soo" was strategically important to the NWC as it was one of the key locations where they diverted Lake Superior furs from their rival Hudson's Bay Company. The small community of Nor'Westers and a few free traders existed almost at a subsistence level. An 1802 letter begged the garrison at Fort St. Joseph to supply them with enough flour and pork to last until spring—too bad that Fort St. Joseph was itself often suffering from a lack of food and supplies.

In July 1814, at the tail end of the War of 1812, 150 American soldiers under the command of Major Arthur Holmes arrived to find both Saults virtually empty. Fur trader John Johnston, though appointed the American Collector of Customs, had gathered a hundred men to help the British protect Fort Michilimackinac from recapture by the Americans. Ironically, the American troops first went to the American side and razed Johnston's home and business. Afterwards they crossed to the Canadian side and burned the North West Company buildings, the lumber mill and a number of homes, and destroyed the lock. They also sent a Nor'Wester schooner the *Perseverance* for a joyride down the rapids, and then burned her once she was snagged on a rock.

Forced to leave Michigan in 1796, the North West Company found the uninhabited Canadian shore a swampland.

The Hudson's Bay Co. post in Sault, Ontario

The Nor'Westers rebuilt their post at a new site beside the bog "into which a careless individual could sink waist deep". Across the river, Johnston failed in an attempt to sue Britain for his losses and so he audaciously tried (and failed) to elicit compensation from the American government. He did receive strange retribution of a sort when an Indian presented his family with Major Holmes' sword, removed from Holmes' corpse after the failed American attack to regain Fort Michilimackinac.

In the ensuing years, Sault Ste. Marie stagnated as the North West Company concentrated its efforts on the more lucrative Drummond Island operation (where British troops had moved after vacating Fort Michilimackinac). In 1821 the Company amalgamated with its rival the Hudson's Bay Company, and henceforth the Lake Superior furs were diverted up to Hudson Bay rather than being sent through the Sault and on to Montreal.

On her trip in 1837, writer Anna Jameson was struck by the disparity between the American and Canadian Saults. After describing American developments, she commented: "Nearly opposite to the American fort there is a small factory belonging to the Fur Company; below this, a few miserable log huts, occupied by some French-Canadian voyageurs in the service of the company, a set of lawless *mauvais sujets*, from all I can learn."

In many ways the Saults considered themselves one community. The border was merely an inconvenience. In one incident in 1838, when the HBC Factor William Nourie feared an attack planned by French and Métis from the American Sault, he crossed the river to enlist assistance from Fort Brady which threatened to shoot, arrest or imprison anyone suspected of anti-British activity. Sault, Ontario was so distant from any Canadian centre that "cross-border shopping" was a necessity, as was reliance on the U.S. postal system. Factor Nourie discovered that this was a potential problem when one had letters of military sensitivity. In 1838, Nourie delayed posting a letter for two weeks, informing his superiors that the trading post had suffered an unprovoked attack from Fort Brady (the garrison had lobbed a few cannonballs across the river that arced over the HBC and imbedded in the hills directly behind). Reprimanded for the delay, Nourie protested that it had taken that long to find a trustworthy Canadian to mail the letter (which was finally done on the Canadian side of the Detroit River). It was not until 1863 that the Canadian Sault was connected to the Penetanguishene mail route.

The only explanation for the Fort Brady assault was that temporary commander, Colonel George Croghan, was still angry towards the British after his failed attempt to recapture Fort Michilimackinac in the War of 1812. The incident was a great embarrassment to the U.S. military because on the whole the two cities were extremely congenial. Even fur traders from competing companies were friendly. However strong the friendships, the Canadian government finally acknowledged that depending on the U.S. infrastructure jeopardized national security.

A CANADIAN SHIP CANAL AND LOCK

Military Mission Blocked By Americans

The mood was sour as the troops prepared their equipment and seventy-pound packs to haul overland while nearby, their ship, the *Chicora*, sat empty. Under Colonel Garnet Joseph Wolseley, the force comprised of British regulars and two detachments from Quebec and Ontario, had departed Collingwood aboard the steamer on May 7, 1870. Their mission was to quell a Métis uprising in Manitoba led by the charismatic Louis Riel. Suspecting the Americans might close the State Lock to military vessels, the *Algoma* was sent ahead with only voyageurs and workmen on board. Although she locked through without incident, soon after an order came from Washington barring all British ships from the American lock. After Canada threatened to close the Welland Canal to American vessels in retaliation, the U. S. partly recanted, but continued to deny access to a British ship on military missions. The *Chicora* was refused passage through.

Colonel Wolseley wasted no time. He established a camp below the rapids and instructed his soldiers to haul their packs and munitions five or six miles through the woods along the old voyageur portage trail. Days later, the empty *Chicora*, removed of everything military, was per-

*Soldiers en route to quell the Riel Rebellion camping after
Americans refused their ship access to the State Lock, 1870.*

mitted to pass through the lock. (However, one story tells
of a brazen soldier who, too lazy to haul his seventy
pound pack overland, hid in the ship's hold.)

   The incident pointed up the importance of a transportation network in maintaining national security.
Canada set about to remedy the weakness of its transportation system and in 1885 completed the "National
Dream," a railway from sea to sea. In 1887 the Canadian
Pacific Railway reached the Sault and in that same year
construction began on a Canadian canal and lock. The
900-foot-long canal, completed in 1895, was among the
first in the world to produce hydro-electricity to operate
its machinery.

Boom and Rescue

   In Sault, Ontario, the arrival of the Canadian Pacific
Railway ushered in a boom. Real estate prices rose and by
1889 the population had reached 1,600. With the com-

pletion of the International Railway Bridge that same year, Michigan had direct access to Canada's transcontinental rail system, further cementing links between the two communities.

It was Judge Steere from Sault, Michigan who came across a reference to an early lock on the Canadian shore while examining old documents. He was intrigued. As far as anyone knew, Americans had been the first to build a lock. His request for copies of early maps sparked the interest of the Superintendent of the American lock and a Canadian provincial land surveyor, Joseph Cozins. Cozins gathered a group of men and started to excavate. It did not take long before they struck a portion of the wooden floor and lock foundation of the North West Company's 1797 lock and boat canal. It was in near perfect condition. What a fitting discovery coming on the heels of the 1887 incorporation of the town that had sprung from the old fur trading post.

Sault, Ontario forged ahead—perhaps too quickly. Hoping to attract manufacturing the city built its own power plant incurring a huge debt. No new businesses came, taxes skyrocketed, population declined, and, adding insult to injury, one of the canal banks gave way. Enter the American-born industrialist Francis Clergue. He assumed the debt in exchange for gaining rights to electric power generation at the rapids. This was just the beginning of his empire. He expanded first into pulpwood then into nickel, iron and steel and finally railroads. At their height, his companies employed about 7,000 people. The expansion had been too rapid, however, and in 1903 his empire collapsed from financial mismanagement exacerbated by labour unrest. Today, his legacy lives on in the Algoma

Central Railway, Algoma Steel Corporation and Great
Lakes Power Company, all of which remain important
employers in the Canadian Sault, now the big sister of the
two Saults.

The Canadian Canal is well worth visiting. Another
interesting fragment of canal history is the portion of the
old 1797 North West Company canal that can still be seen
downtown near the river. For a glimpse into the fur trade,
visit the Ermatinger Old Stone House. Nearby is the
Hudson's Bay Company's Blockhouse, reconstructed by
Clergue as his residence around 1900. The Sault Ste.
Marie Museum has fascinating displays that interpret
Algoma's history.

Francis Clergue's blockhouse and two pet bears

PICTURE CREDITS

Archives de la Province du Canada Français, Saint-
Jerome, Quebec:32,34
Archives of Ontario:41,62,128,193,
Archives Jesuit Fathers,Upper Canada:47,109,111,248
Bayliss Public Library:(R)259
Bruce Mines Museum & Archives:XXXV,179,183
Cape Croker First Nation:21
Chicago Historical Society:260
Chippewa County Historical Society:243,245
Cook, S.F., *Drummond Island: Story of the British
Occupation*:207
DeTour Passage Historical Museum:212
Drummond Island Museum:166
Goertzville, Raber, Lime Island Centennial Book: 232
Gore Bay Museum, Gore Bay:55,56,70,73,80,101,292
Great Lakes Historical Society:265
J. & E. Estelle, *River of Destiny*:261
J. & E. Estelle, *Historic St. Joseph Island*:162
Huronia Museum:(Bev Keefe Collection)8(James Barry
Collection)150
Kauffman, *Blind River Logging Days*:133,135
Library of Congress:224
McKenny Tour of the Lakes: Hambleton Colln.:(L)259
McMichael Canadian Art Collection Archives/ Joachim
Gauthier:14
Mer Douce:58,92
Metro Toronto Reference Library, Baldwin Rm: XVII,
XXIV, 87, 272, 275
Metro Toronto Reference Library: XIV, XXXVI, XXXIX,

3, 77, 108, 120,130,177,204,237,253,255,267,269,277
Michigan Department of Natural Resources:229, 231,
National Archives of Canada:XXIII, XXXIX, 77, 143,
148, 160, 209
National Library of Canada:271
Otto Fowle, *Sault Ste.Marie and its Great Waterway*: XXX
Sault Ste. Marie Museum, Ontario:256
St. Joseph Island Museum Village:187,195,198
J. E. MacDonald, *This Point of Land*:173
Timber Village Museum:134
J. E. MacDonald, *Yonder Our Island*:152
YMCA, Sudbury:114,115
MacDonald J. E., *Yonder Our Island*:

Individual Collections:
Ron Brown:105
Jennylee Church Olesek:274
Norman Lloyd:65,98
Janet Looker:39,52,216
Lyle Marcellus:124,125
Ken McColman:83
Donald McKenzie:49
Harold McQuarrie:155, 156, 171
Michael Mulloy: 263
Rosalie Sasso:169
Leonard & Merle Solomon:6
Dorothy Spreadborough-Wilkins:16
Merritt Strum:XXXI
John Wellington:214
Across fr title pg: Bruce Mines Museum & Archives
Across from disclaimer: Harold McQuarrie

SELECTED BIBLIOGRAPHY

Albert, M. *Trade History: North Shore of Lake Huron*. Iron
    Bridge, Ont.: Rae's North Country Printing, 1996.

Arbic, Bernard. *Sugar Island Sampler*, Sault Ste. Marie: Privately
    printed, 1993.

Ashley, K. Beldon. *Islands of the Manitou*. Florida, Coral Gables.
    Fla.: Crystal Bay Publishers, 1985.

Barber, M. *The Formative Years of Bruce Mines: A Social
    History*. Bruce Mines Museum and Archives, 1991.

Barry, James. *Georgian Bay: The Sixth Great* Lake. Toronto:
    Clarke, Irwin & Co. Ltd., 1968.

_____ .*Ships of the Great Lakes*. Lansing, MI: Thunder Bay
    Press, 1996.

Bayliss, Joseph and Estelle. *Historic St. Joseph Island*. Cedar
    Rapids: Torch Press, 1938.

_____. *River of Destiny*. Detroit: Wayne
    University. Press, 1955.

Berton, Pierre. *The Invasion of Canada* 1812-1813. Toronto:
    McClelland and Stewart, 1980.

Bigsby, J. *The Shoe and the Canoe*. Chapman and Hall, 1850.

Brazer, M. Cahan. *Well Favoured Passage*. Toronto: Peter Martin
    and Assoc.,1975.

Callan, Kevin. *Killarney*. Erin, Ont.:Boston Mills, 1990.

Cook, S.F. *Drummond Island: Story of the British Occupation*.
    Lansing, MI: R. Smith Printing Co., 1896.

Cross, Paul. *Ferry Fare*. Drummond Island, MI: Drummond
    Island Beacon Journal, 1989.

Eccles, W.J. *The Canadian Frontier (1534-1760)*. Univ. of New
    Mexico Press, 1983.

Edward, J. "Lime Island Happenings", Great Lakes Cruiser. May 1996.

Fowle, Otto. *Sault Ste. Marie and its Great Waterway*. New York: G.P. Putnam's Sons, 1925.

Frost, Rev. F. *Sketches of Indian Life*. Toronto: W. Briggs, 1904.

Greenman, E.F. *Old Birch Island Cemetery*. Ann Arbor: Univ. of Michigan Press, 1951.

Gutsche, A. *Alone in the Night*. Toronto:Lynx Images, 1996.

_____.*Ghosts of the Bay*. Toronto: Lynx Images, 1994.

Hornick, J. *The Call for Copper*. Bruce Mines: Peer Printing, 1969.

Jameson, Anna B. *Winter Studies and Summer Rambles*. Toronto: McClelland & Stewart, 1990.

Johnston, Basil. *Indian School Days*. Toronto: Key Porter Books, 1988

Kauffmann, C. *Logging Days in Blind River*. Sault Ste. Marie, Ont.: Sault Star Commercial Printing, 1970.

Kohl, Cris. *Dive Ontario*! Chatham, Ont.: Privately printed, 1990.

Landon, Fred. *Lake Huron*. Indianapolis: Bobbs-Merrill, 1944.

Lay, Gregory. *Memories of Early Days on St. Joseph's Island*. Kirkland Lake, Ont.:Sutherland Printing House.

MacDonald, J.E. *This Point of Land*. Sault Ste. Marie, Ont., 1977.

MacDonald, J.E. *Yonder Our Island*. Township of Cockburn I sland, 1979.

Major F.W. *Manitoulin Island of the Ottawas*. Gore Bay, Ont., 1934.

Martin, Bruce. *The Island of St. Joseph and St. Mary's River*. Echo Bay, Ontario: Words Unlimited, 1991.

Mer Douce. The Algonquin Historical Society, vol. 1-12 (May

1921-Sept. 1932).

Mount, Graeme; Abbott, John; Mulloy, Michael. *The Border at Sault Ste. Marie*. Toronto: Dundurn Press, 1995.

Myers, Frank. "Reprint of Articles Copied for the Manitoulin Historical Society". Manitoulin Is., Ont., 1956.

Newman, Peter. *Caesars of the Wilderness*. Markham, Ont.: Penguin Books, 1987.

_____. *Company of Adventurers*. Markham, Ont.: Penguin Books, 1985.

Pearen, Shelley. *Exploring Manitoulin*. Toronto: University of Toronto Press, 1993.

Prestwood, L. *The Canadian War of 1812*. Oxford: Clarendon Press, 1906.

Quinby, G. *Indian Life in the Upper Great Lakes*. Chicago: University of Chicago Press, 1960.

Rains, J. *St. Joseph Island a Tour and Historical Guide*. Journal Printing, 1988.

Schmalz, Peter. *The Ojibwe of Southern Ontario*. Toronto: University of Toronto Press, 1991.

Smith, Hermon Dunlap. "The Desbarats Country". Chicago: Privately printed, 1950.

Smith, Theresa. *The Island of the Anishnaabeg*. Idaho: University of Idaho Press, 1995.

Tanner, H. H. *The Ojibwa*. Chelsea House Publishers, 1992.

_____ *Atlas of Great Lakes Indian History*, Norman, Oklahoma, Univ of Oklahoma Press, 1987.

Wells, K.M. *Cruising the North Channel*. Toronto: Kingswood House, 1960.

ACKNOWLEDGEMENTS

This book could not have been compiled without the generous assistance of the following individuals. While many have contributed to the project, any errors or omissions found in the text are ours alone.

We would like to extend our gratitude to those who shared their experiences and memories: Corella Corbiere, David Corbiere, Garry Green, Frank Crowder, Esther Jacko, Joe Lowe, Lyle Marcellus, Margaret McKay, Ken "Nine-Lives" McColman, George McGregor, Merrill Moore, Charlie Quinn, "Trapper Jim" Reed, Rosalie Sasso, Ron Showan, Norman Smith, Dorothy Spreadborough-Wilkins, and Ivan Trick.

Our sincere appreciation goes to the individuals at museums, libraries, Band offices and other institutions on whom we relied extensively: John Abbott, Algoma University College; Marion Albert, and Christine Clark, Curator, Timber Village Museum, Blind River, for lending us the extensive research collected for *Trade History of the North Shore*; Esther Jacko, Chief Leona Nahwegahbow, and Council at Whitefish River First Nation; Merritt Strum (you're a prince, Merritt!); Gail Tisdale, Curator, St. Joseph Island Museum Village; Byron Turner for sharing his historical research; Nicole Weppler, Curator, Gore Bay Museum; and Russ Woods.

Others who assisted our research and picture gathering were: Bernie Arbic, Archives of Ontario; Bayliss Public Library; Mary Bockman, Thessalon Library; Darryl Boissoneau, Garden River

First Nation; Bruce Mines Museum and Archives; Ray Corbiere; John Cywink; Doug and Bobby Diamond; Drummond Island Museum; Father Boyle, Jesuit Archives, Toronto; Stoney Burton, Manager Blind River Ministry of Culture, Recreation and Tourism; Peggy Chapman; Adam Debassige, West Bay First Nation; Gary Gray, YMCA Sudbury; Darlene Johnston, Cape Croker First Nation; Debby Haight; Shawn Heissler; Carol Hiney, DeTour Area Highschool; Ossie Hunt; Linda Kelly, Curator, Little Current-Howland Museum, Sheguiandah; Debbie Maiangowi, Wikwemikong Unceded Indian Reserve; Judy McGonigal, Curator, Sault Ste. Marie Museum, Ont.; Harold McQuarrie; Jack McQuarrie; Metro Toronto Reference Library; Net Shed Museum, Meldrum Bay; Jennylee Church Olesek; Peggy Phelps; River of History Museum, Sault MI; Bill Smith, Huronia Museum; Aaron, Len, and Merle Solomon; Dr. Peter Storck and Dr. Peter Von Bitter, Royal Ontario Museum; Elna Van Houten, Curator, DeTour Passage Historical Museum; John Wellington; Ann Wilson, Michigan Department of Natural Resources and Willard Witty.

And to those who worked in the trenches, thank you: our editor, Barbara D. Chisholm for her many hours and clear thinking; R. W. Chisholm; Deborah Wise Harris for meticulous copy editing; Jo-Ey Lee for cover design and picture repair; Janet Looker, artist-in-residence; and to Charlie for living with files.

INDEX

Winter mail delivery, Little Current

ABOUT THE AUTHORS

Barbara Chisholm, Russell Floren, and Andrea Gutsche are the three partners of Lynx Images, a unique company that combines filmmaking and book publishing as a means to explore and document vanishing pieces of Canadian history. Their previous books and films, *Ghosts of the Bay*, *Alone in the Night*, *Superior Under the shadow of the Gods*, *Mysterious Islands* and *Castles of the North* are all Canadian bestsellers.

Other titles in the Lynx Images catalogue include *Enchanted Summers*, *Disaster Great Lakes* and *Disaster Canada*

The upcoming film about lost *Newfoundland, Vanished in the Mist*, has a 2003 release.

Andrea Gutsche and Russell Floren on board the Upper Lakes Shipping freighter, Canadian Leader.

GHOSTS OF THE BAY

The Forgotten History of Georgian Bay
Guide Book and Video

The 90-minute film leads viewers on an expedition to the haunting vestiges of Georgian Bay's past (now an eerie world of shipwrecks, ghost towns, fishing camps, lumber villages, and native sites). The Bay's story comes alive through archival film, photographs, character voices, and stunning underwater cinematography. Bring the book along on your own journey, and transform your experience of Georgian Bay. The 300-page book includes 140 sites, 50 maps, and fascinating archival photographs. 92 minute video/300-page book

0-9698427-1-6   Bk/Video $49.95
0-9698427-0-8   Video $29.95
0-9698427-3-2   Book $24.95

ALONE IN THE NIGHT

Lighthouses of Georgian Bay, Manitoulin Island
and the North Channel
Book and video

Lighthouses capture the imagination with their fascinating stories and forgotten memories. Together the book and 72-minute video return you to a time when the Great Lakes were the lifeblood of the country. *Alone in the Night* traces the evolution of lightkeeping, revealing the heroic and the scandalous, the gritty and the routine aspects of this remarkable chapter of Canada's marine heritage. Over 50 lighthouse sites, letting the stories, photographs, and maps transform your trip into an unforgettable journey.

300-page book/72-minute video
0-9698427-4-0   Book/Video $49.95
0-9698427-6-7   Video $29.95
0-9698427-5-9   Book $34.95

SUPERIOR: UNDER THE SHADOW OF THE GODS

Book and video

The history of Lake Superior's magnificent Canadian shore is explored in all its drama in this remarkable book and film. The book follows the Canadian shore from Sault Ste. Marie north past Thunder Bay to the American border. Past and present are linked through historical stories, ghost towns, shipwrecks and other fascinating abandoned sites. The book includes over 200 sites, maps and archival photographs.

The breathtaking film reveals Lake Superior as a world belonging to the gods. The human experience here is one of challenge; our attempts to exploit this place have left ghost towns and other fading marks on these wild and rugged shores. Rare archival footage and photographs, voices from the past, stunning cinematography, and a haunting score enrich these compelling sagas.

72 minute video/320-page book
0-9698427-9-1 Bk/Video $49.95
0-9698427-8-3 Video $29.95
0-9698427-7-5 Book $24.95

DISASTER GREAT LAKES

Violent, unpredictable weather has brought down ships from War of 1812 schooners to the legendary Edmund Fitzgerald. On shore, great fires have devastated the young cities of Chicago and Toronto, and cut huge swaths through the forests leaving thousands dead or homeless. Train wrecks, explosions and environmental disasters such as the Love Canal have become painful catalysts of change.

The human core in all its complexity is revealed by the many compelling ways people respond in times of crisis. Richly told and illustrated, this book includes a concise list of the worst catastrophes in the history of the Great Lakes region, both American and Canadian.
ISBN 1-894073-26-6 $24.95

OTHER TITLES FROM LYNX IMAGES

MYSTERIOUS ISLANDS:
Forgotten Tales of the Great Lakes

An island ruled by a king who declared it his own country, an island used as a hideout by a notorious pirate, an island mined by pre-historic copper miners... these are only a few of the stories in this remarkable collection.

The book and film, *Mysterious Islands*, is a fascinating historical journey to islands in the vast basin of the five Great Lakes. Islands have been central to some of the most important, outrageous and tragic events in Great Lakes history, from a battle in the War of 1812, to Prohibition rumrunning, to harrowing tales of shipwreck and rescue. The waves of time have left many islands behind, but remnants of the past still mark their shores- burial grounds, grand hotels, abandoned quarries, lighthouses, strategic forts, and even a castle. Indispensable for boaters, this guide book is brimming with stories of island names, shipwrecks, abandoned places, folklore and intrigue.

296 pages, photos & illus. softcover

ISBN 1-894073-12-6
Book and Video $49.95
ISBN 1-894073-11-8
Book $24.95
ISBN 1-894073-10-x
Video $29.95

12 Weeks on Canadian-Bestsellers list

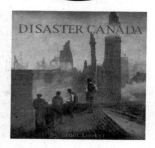

Sobering, inspiring, shocking and instructive!
-London Free Press

DISASTER CANADA
Disasters From the 1700s to Present Day

DISASTER CANADA travels across the country from its rough beginnings to the present, exploring the history of its most devastating catastrophes.

In this book, stories and dramatic photographs expose the human core; our will to survive, our heroism, and our capacity to face the worst. Beneath the shock of the headlines lies the rich story of Canada's sometimes painful growth, a nation that time after time has pulled together in crisis. Covers 70 disasters from the 1700s to the year 2000. The book also includes a comprehensive list of over 100 Canadian disasters and over 200 black and white photographs, maps and diagrams.

288-pages, soft-cover ISBN 1894073134 $24.95

Lynx Images Inc., PO Box 5961, Sta A, Toronto, ON   M5W 1P4
Ph: (416) 925-8422 Fax: (416) 925-8352 email: orders@lynximages.com
Visit our Website www.lynximages.com